METROPOLITAN FINANCING

Metropolitan Financing

The Milwaukee Experience, 1920–1970

Donald J. Curran

THE UNIVERSITY OF WISCONSIN PRESS

Published 1973
The University of Wisconsin Press
Box 1379, Madison, Wisconsin 53701

The University of Wisconsin Press, Ltd.
70 Great Russell Street, London

First printing

Printed in the United States of America

For LC CIP information see the colophon
ISBN 0–299–06290–2

To Jennie

Contents

Tables

Preface

RARELY, if ever, does a metropolitan study end on an optimistic note. The conclusions are invariably dreary. This is true of metropolitan investigations in general; it is especially true of those that focus on taxes and related fiscal matters.

How can one explain, then, the fact that so very little has been done to change things? The answer to that question may well go beyond the usual explanations of popular apathy and the stake that public officials have in retaining the status quo. It may even go beyond the oft-repeated truism that the average person finds it difficult to look beyond issues like the expansion of the local junior high school or the recent increases in his property taxes. The real answer may be rooted in human psychology. Many people apparently want to believe that "the metropolitan problem" is getting better, and this could be the reason so little attention is paid to pessimistic reports.

It is conceivable that this wishful thinking could be correct. Maybe things are getting better. Perhaps this fond hope is well grounded. Only an historical investigation can tell for certain. To find out, this study was undertaken. Because urban and metropolitan ills seem to be especially acute in older northern areas, one of them should be chosen for examination. Since New York and Chicago are thought to be unique because of their size, they wouldn't do. Since Boston and Philadelphia are special cases because of sheer age, they wouldn't do. Milwaukee was chosen. It is marvellously typical. If the problem seems to be solving itself in the Milwaukee metropolitan area, there is basis for hope. If the problem is worsening there, it is probably worsening in most of the other big urban areas.

In public finance literature, no other study was found that tried to follow the trend of metropolitan finances over a significant period of time—in this case, over a span of 50 years (1920–1970). The state of Wisconsin, true to its well-deserved reputation, provided the data to make an evolutionary fiscal study possible and rewarding.

Chapter 8 appeared in *Land Economics;* other portions of the book appeared in the *National Tax Journal.* I am grateful to editors of both journals for permission to use those materials here.

This study owes much to the late Professor Harold M. Groves of the University of Wisconsin—Madison. I can only repeat what I said about Mr. Groves on the Acknowledgments page of my doctoral dissertation about a decade ago: "He filled all the professor's roles of teaching, guiding, sharing, helping—and he filled them well. But he did more. By being what he is, he has communicated to me a high sense of purpose and a high ideal of what the Public Finance Economist can be and can do."

Cleveland, Ohio   D. J. C.
June, 1972

METROPOLITAN
FINANCING

1 The Question

THERE IS an urban crisis in America. The press, government officials, the business community, the black community, the general public, and even academicians agree on this point.

Racial friction has helped to focus attention on the problems of the cities. But even before the surfacing of white-black issues, the large cities were in deep trouble. And long after racial violence has, I hope, ended, the big cities will continue to deteriorate. For one thing, extra tax burdens will still hurt the older cities.[1] The transportation tangle will continue to plague cities more and more. The movement of business (both industrial and commercial firms) out of cities is destined not merely to continue but to quicken. Nearly all of the critical elements in today's headlines (education, welfare, slums, poverty, unemployment) may become less volatile without racial antagonism but not less real and pressing.

There is no need mercilessly to repeat the list of big city sore spots; they have been extensively publicized and are known to all. The question now is what to do about the urban crisis. One recurring suggestion is that the situation can and should be met on the metropolitan level. That is, since most of the large cities where the sickness is acute turn out to be the hubs of surrounding suburbs, the malady should

1. Dick Netzer, *Economics of the Property Tax* (Washington: The Brookings Institution, 1966), p. 75.

be dealt with as an areawide problem. "For these central cities, though they are an inseparable segment of a larger metropolitan organism in a social and economic sense, are yet a separable entity in the taxing, spending and regulating sense."[2] A metropolitan approach to the problem might involve functional coordination (e.g., an areawide school or transportation system); or it might involve cooperation (e.g., a voluntary common effort of all the counties, cities, villages, and towns of the region to deal with an issue like air and water pollution); or it might involve revenue sharing (e.g., an areawide sales tax that would be shared by each of the municipalities); or it might involve actual political integration (e.g., creation of a super-government to run the entire metropolitan area).

A second alternative is for state governments to assume greater responsibility for large cities. Some who have worked closely with state governments smile at this suggestion. Nonetheless, in spite of the lassitude of many state legislatures, and in spite of the fact that the much-heralded "one-man —one-vote" decision has apparently not enhanced the clout of large cities at the state capital,[3] the plight of the cities has received some state recognition. This alternative would involve more recognition. For example, the state might take over some of the functions that put unusually heavy burdens on big cities. Or, more generous state aids could be provided to large cities. Again, the state might use its sovereign power to directly or indirectly reorganize governmental units at the local level (e.g., by permitting cities to annex more freely,

2. Raymond Vernon, *The Changing Economic Function of the Central City* (New York: Committee for Economic Development, 1959), pp. 13, 14 (quotation).

3. Walter Heller correctly reminds us that, even after reapportionment, "central cities will be represented in proportion, not to their problems, but to their population. They cannot solve the crushing problems of poverty, racial disability, obsolete social capital, pollution, and undernourished public services from revenues drawn from their own limited tax bases." Walter W. Heller, et al., *Revenue Sharing and the City* (Baltimore: The Johns Hopkins Press), p. 32.

by changing charter powers, etc.). Finally, the state might deal with the sickness of large cities by imposing one of the metropolitan forms mentioned above.

The federal government is another source of possible relief for the large city illness.[4] It is no secret that Washington has increased its ties with cities enormously since World War II. It has been primarily through the grant-in-aid mechanism; many urban problems that had previously been neglected are now being dealt with, thanks to federal initiative (e.g., housing, urban renewal, expressways, mass transit studies, airports, anti-poverty programs, hospital construction, etc.).[5] Perhaps this flow of funds from Washington to the cities can be expanded. Another approach would be federal assumption of financial responsibility for functions that now strain some city budgets. Examples might be welfare, compensatory education, health care, pollution control, etc. Still a further possibility would be some form of revenue sharing—a simple unconditional channeling of funds to the cities from Washington. All these proposals for more aid to cities from the state or the federal capital raise familiar questions about loss of local independence and about the death of grass roots government. A major concern of this study is the validity of or justification for local autonomy in a metropolitan context.

There is another alternative: can the cities not handle their current problems from within? Can the cities not find inside their own borders the resources required for satisfactory housing, education, jobs, police protection, transportation, care of the elderly and indigent, health, sanitation, and so forth? After all, a large part of the wealth of the nation is in the cities. To put it another way, why go through the roundabout and costly process of having the state or federal government raise money from city taxpayers and then use it for city needs? This question, plausible though it sounds, misses many facets

4. Roscoe C. Martin, *The Cities and the Federal System* (New York: Atherton Press, 1965). That there should be and will be a growing relationship of federal aid to cities is a theme of this work.

5. Donald J. Curran, "Federal-Local Financial Relations," *Review of Social Economy* 25 (September 1967):183–95.

of the urban fiscal malaise. For one thing, cities are much constrained by state restrictions (both constitutional and statutory) in the types and amounts of taxes they may employ. At present, most local taxes are property taxes. Property tax rates in large cities—especially in the older ones—are disproportionately high; they generally run well above those in surrounding suburban communities. Speaking of property tax rates in general, Joseph Pechman of the Brookings Institution said a few years ago, "In many cities and towns, property tax rates are already too high and further substantial increases in these rates are both unlikely and undesirable."[6] How about nonproperty taxes? Large cities use them much more intensively than other local governments. In 1967, five of the six cities with populations over 1,000,000 and 15 of the 25 cities with populations over 500,000 had either a local sales tax or an income tax or both.[7] They stacked these taxes right on top of their unusually high property taxes, despite the fear of thereby speeding up the flight of residents and business firms out of big cities. Empirical studies of the influence of local taxes on business location suggest that this fear is exaggerated, but Laszlo Ecker-Racz's comment remains valid: "although the influence of tax considerations on the location decisions of business is grossly overstated, . . . its impact on state and local taxation is not. . . . Fear of losing business to another jurisdiction haunts the mind and stills the pen of the state and local lawmaker, and special pleaders have developed the skill of exploiting this fear to a high art."[8] The purpose of mentioning all this is to rebut the ill-founded charge that the current critical situation of cities is the result

6. Joseph Pechman, in a paper prepared for the Symposium of Federal Taxation of the American Bankers' Association, March 26, 1965.

7. Advisory Commission on Intergovernmental Relations, *Tax Overlapping in the United States: Selected Tables Updated: A Supplement to Report M-23* (Washington: ACIR, 1968).

8. L. L. Ecker-Racz, "Fiscal Crisis in an Affluent Society," in *City Problems of 1966*, The Annual Proceedings of the United States Conference of Mayors, pp. 103–9.

of their unwillingness to use their own resources.[9] Another convenient myth that deserves a firm burial is that urban problems can be traced to the inefficiency, graft, patronage, and indifference of local officials. In general, these men have responded to growing problems with imagination and courage. In spite of an honest (and often frantic) effort to meet demands made on them, however, and in spite of stretching their revenue-raising powers to perilous limits, city governments and their officials have not been able to keep pace. A solution must be sought elsewhere.

In a sense, there is one final alternative. The nation can let the situation continue to deteriorate. Despite dire warnings by countless scholars and commissions, that is the avenue we have been following. Nonetheless, concern over poverty and race may conceivably evoke a change of direction. In such an event, which of the foregoing approaches shows the most promise? Solution at the state level offers little encouragement. A mixture of elements—inertia, fear of driving out business, the composition of state legislatures, the growing centralization of our whole economy—make this alternative a weak reed on which to lean. How about the cities raising themselves by their own bootstraps? As noted in the preceding paragraph, further fiscal efforts by the cities themselves would almost surely be self-defeating. That leaves the paths of metropolitan coordination and of federal intervention. Before taking the federal route, one wonders if there is any hope at all at the metropolitan level. To explore that possibility, this study of the Milwaukee metropolitan area was undertaken. It seeks to find out whether the metropolitan problem shows any signs of solving itself.

There are metropolitan problems, and there is "the metropolitan problem." The former are legion in number; among them are uneven tax burdens, unequal public service levels, spillovers, inefficiencies, etc. The latter is single and all-inclu-

9. This point is well covered and well documented by Joseph R. Fahey, "Advisability and Probable Economic Effects of a Local Income or Local Sales Tax in Boston" (Ph.D. Diss., Massachusetts Institute of Technology, 1966).

sive: the problem of economic unity fractured by political multiplicity.[10] Further, this splintering has become increasingly recognized as the fertile spawning-bed of the former difficulties, especially of spillovers (i.e., the benefits that "spill over" the boundaries of the municipality paying for them into other municipalities which escape the tax costs). As long as the single economic base of a metropolitan area is split into odd-shaped governmental pieces, the problem of spillovers will remain.

Fiscal disparities (differences in tax resources, in tax rates, and in levels of public spending) are a critical feature of metropolitanism. These disparities are both part of the metropolitan problem and also a major motive for not solving the problem. The motivational aspect is a matter of fiscal self-interest. Those municipalities with an extra large tax base naturally want to preserve it. Those with high levels of educational quality similarly want to maintain that condition. The same is true of those with unusually low tax rates. They all have strong reasons for keeping the metropolitan area splintered. They all have reasons for fighting against areawide taxes or any other kind of coordination. To expect local officials to work for the common good of the metropolitan area to the detriment of their individual municipalities is not only wishful thinking but would also involve a betrayal of their responsibilities to the people who elected them. It is not the individual locality that is to be condemned for this narrow self-interest but rather the governmental system that assigns to a metropolitan municipality the same roles as it does to an isolated, nonmetropolitan municipality.

The crucial role of these fiscal disparities, therefore, suggests an important question: are fiscal differences among metropolitan municipalities lessening over time? If the answer is affirmative, then part of the metropolitan problem itself

10. "On the one hand, a metropolis is a single economic unit—huge and sprawling though it may be. On the other, it is a highly complicated network of individual governments, of competing interests, and of conflicting prejudices." James A. Norton, *Prologue to Progress* (Cleveland: Cleveland Metropolitan Services Commission, 1959), p. 1.

is improving and the barriers to solving other parts of the problem are dissolving. As a small contribution toward an answer to the question, an investigation was made of the Milwaukee Metropolitan Area. The documentation for an answer appears in Chapters 4–8; the answer itself is discussed in Chapter 9.

The most casual observer is aware that fiscal considerations (government taxing and spending) constitute only some of the threads in the web of attitudes and motivations keeping metropolitan municipalities apart. There is no intention here even to argue that fiscal elements are the major threads in this fabric. Yet all agree that they are significant. To that extent, fiscal trends are worth studying.

The study has relevance far beyond the borders of the Milwaukee Metropolitan Area. It is fortunate that this central city and the surrounding suburban area are quite typical of their American counterparts. Milwaukee is also typical in the sense that it is a large city deeply embroiled in the urban crisis.

2 The Approach

Financial Approach

THIS IS a financial study. Government taxing, spending, and borrowing at the local level are being put under the microscope. One who understands in depth how the local governments of a metropolitan area raise and spend their funds has gone a long way towards comprehending the metropolitan problem. More specifically, in terms of the central hypothesis of this investigation, local public finances can shed considerable light on the question of how much voluntary metropolitan coordination can be expected.

From the viewpoint of a local taxpayer (whether an individual, a family, a store, an office, or a factory), there is an understandable concern about property tax rates. Of perhaps greater concern to the taxpayer is how the tax revenues are spent. In particular, what kind of schools does the village or city have? This has been found to be a major determinant of where people choose to live.[1] A place for the children to play, recreational facilities (parks, playgrounds, swimming pools), traffic conditions, presence or absence of public housing developments, nearness of heavy industry, high or low crime rates—all these environmental aspects, which are inexorably tied to a municipality's budget, also loom large in choosing a place to live.

1. Raymond Vernon, *Metropolis 1985* (Cambridge, Mass.: Harvard University Press, 1960), p. 147.

Since these budgetary items mean so much to a resident, control over them will not be readily surrendered. In that sense, financial considerations may pose a significant barrier to any real coming together of metropolitan localities. If differences in the financial profiles of municipalities are large, there exists for some a clear incentive to retain the present splintering. On the other hand, the more that metropolitan communities resemble one another in their tax levels, tax rates, expenditure patterns, and quality of public service, the more likely they are to agree voluntarily to some form of functional or political coordination.

To be sure, nonfinancial barriers exist, and they are not to be lightly dismissed. There is the loyalty a resident feels toward Fox Point, or Orchard Park, or San Francisco. There is the vested interest of local officials. There is the attachment to home rule, to government close to the people. There is the prestige associated with a particular town or village. There is the deep desire to live in a certain kind of environment, among certain kinds of neighbors. But it seems safe to predict that these barriers would yield somewhat more readily if there were not significant disparities in public finances. The question, therefore, whether there is evidence of growing fiscal homogeneity within a metropolitan area is truly a question about possible solutions from within.

Further, it must be recalled that it was deterioration of central cities that largely prompted this examination of the Milwaukee Metropolitan Area. Herein lies a further advantage of doing a financial study. "If the implicit hypothesis that a metropolitan area is a particular type of social-economic-political community is true, then it follows that the finances of the central city or the finances of any of the other parts of the area cannot be understood fully unless the total situation is examined."[2] Mayor Lindsay had a few years of experience in Gracie Mansion behind him when he said, "At the risk of sounding simplistic, it seems to me that all of the

2. Seymour Sacks, Leo M. Egand, William F. Hellmuth, Jr., *The Cleveland Metropolitan Area—A Fiscal Profile* (Cleveland: Cleveland Metropolitan Services Commission, 1958), p. iv.

urban problems can be incorporated in one basic problem, and that is money."[3] To this, the mayors of our large cities say, "Amen."

The tax problems of central cities are legion. Property tax burdens of large cities are unusually high and their per capita tax levels (property and nonproperty) are unusually heavy. State restriction of taxing powers adds to the bind. City officials shake their heads worriedly about raising tax rates as they watch the exodus of people and business from the city. They beg the state for more aids; they go hat in hand to Washington in desperation. Let the political theorists or constitutional lawyers worry about the implications for federalism; the big city mayors must worry about money.

And what do the large cities have to show for their scramble after funds? They have substandard housing and slums; they have old school buildings; they have transportation crises and traffic congestion; they have dirt in the air and in the streets; they have high police costs coupled with high crime rates; they have a disproportionate number of the poor, of the underprivileged, of the elderly, of the unemployed. In short, from a study of local finances in a metropolitan area, one learns not a little about the big city crisis.

Historical Approach

But why a historical study? The main reason is clear enough. An historical approach is the only possible way to test the major hypothesis: there has been an increasing uniformity in the public finances of the localities in the Milwaukee Metropolitan Area over the past 50 years. Which simply means that this evolutionary approach is also the only possible way of testing to see whether there is greater or less likelihood of the area solving its own problems and whether metropolitan coordination looks like a promising way out of the central city stalemate.

Another reason for approaching the metropolitan survey

3. Mayor John Lindsay of New York City in an address in Buffalo, as quoted in the *New York Times*, 26 April, 1968.

historically is the very fact that it is different. In a field of investigation as important as this, every new approach almost automatically has merit. In place of deductive reasoning about spending, one can observe in the local records the fiscal impact of installing a new sewer system, the influence of industrial growth on costs of fire protection, the effect that transition from rural to urban conditions has on per capita expenditures, the expenditure shifts that accompany population density, etc.

Also, the newness of this type of investigation has an educational effect on the people of the area. That is, history helps them to really "see" the heart of the metropolitan problem as no amount of rhetoric can do. The mere unfolding of the evidence demonstrates how the economic unity and economic interdependence of the metropolitan area kept growing while the political, financial, and legal structures failed to adjust. To actually watch the process whereby this splintered unity develops and spreads—and hardens—is convincing.

The time-series method makes it possible to distinguish and examine three types of influences entering into the public finances of municipalities: factors common to all local jurisdictions and affecting them all at the same point of time; factors common to all but affecting them at different points of time; and factors peculiar to one or another locality. The first type of influence includes the depression of the 1930s, the war of the 1940s, the continued prosperity of the post-war era. These influences affected the property tax base, the tax rate, and the expenditure pattern of each and every metropolitan community, and affected them in the same general way, but to decidedly different degrees.

There was a second set of influences that operated on all of the localities but not all at the same time. One of the clearest examples is the huge expense of installing a sewer system and of supplying water. Each of these is a major capital outlay and, at one time or another, each locality, if it undergoes any degree of urbanization at all, has to supply such services. The city of Milwaukee, which was incorporated in 1846 and already had several hundred thousand people in the early part of this century, had supplied its basic sewer and water facilities before this study began. As new sections of the city developed or as new areas were annexed by the central city, it was a relatively small task to extend existing facilities. Far different was the experience of the eight localities which incorporated after 1950. Many of them were faced with the horrendous task of supplying such facilities almost overnight.

But then, too, in the historical evolution of a locality there is a third type of influence that has its effect on the fiscal evolution of one locality but not on its neighbor. Such, for example, is the enormous utility plant recently constructed in the city of Oak Creek. Similarly, the fact that Greendale was originally a federal experimental village puts its development entirely in a class by itself. Because all of the property in that village was once owned by the federal government, its fiscal evolution followed a path distinct from the others.

Distinguishing these various types of influence from one another is not just a pleasant academic exercise; it provides insight into the great variations found today, while also enabling the planner to anticipate the future development of the fringe areas constantly being added to the metropolitan area. This is particularly true of the second type of influence; namely, large capital outlays that each locality must make at some time in its urbanization process. Ability to correlate such spending with specific variables (rates of population growth, density, etc.) gives some basis for predictions about new areas that still have the process of urbanization ahead of them.

A further reason for doing this study in an historical manner was the desire to have a more reliable picture of the area; a 50-year view of the metropolitan area gives a kind of sureness and security that cannot be had in a one-year or a two-year study. With such a long period of time, most of the individual abnormalities and even individual errors (whether in the records or perhaps the tabulation work) are pretty well ironed out, since no one figure is that influential. At the same time, mistakes, or oddities can be more easily discovered and explained. The increased reliability is especially important in Milwaukee County because of the very numerous boundary changes that have taken place through annexations, consolidations, incorporations, etc. That is, practically any year in recent decades is an "unusual" year for some of the localities because of area changes. The only way to sort out the temporary aberrations from the normal pattern is to view each locality over time.

An historical study provides a trustworthy basis for forecasting.[4] An illustration may be helpful. There has been a trend on the part of many localities since World War II to zone significant parts of their land area for large-lot residential uses. This is a relatively new phenomenon and one which will have far-reaching results in the future for taxable values, for rapid transit, for the availability of low income workers, etc. Closely related to this recent trend toward large-lot zoning is a notable increase in specialization of land use. That is, numerous localities within Milwaukee County have used their zoning and planning powers to choose one particular kind of land use to the exclusion of others. As a result, there are highly industrialized suburbs, very wealthy residential suburbs, moderately wealthy residential suburbs, etc. The tendency is definitely away from the balanced land uses found in the central city and the older suburbs. The results for Milwaukee County are serious, and intelligent forecasts based on this trend are quite necessary.

As to policy, the focus of history improves the potential for sound decisions by highlighting the unique characteristics of an area.[5] After summarizing the results of more than a hundred separate metropolitan surveys, one report concluded

4. In speaking of the limitations of regional input-output analysis, one author notes: "Thus, it is often argued that an understanding of basic historical trends and forces is more essential to making good projections than accurate interindustry and interregional trade coefficients." John R. Meyer, "Regional Economics: A Survey," *American Economic Review* 53 (March, 1963):35.

5. Elliott R. Morss, "Some Thoughts on the Determinants of State and Local Expenditures," *National Tax Journal* 19 (March 1966):100.

that the peculiar features of each area were a major influence on policy recommendations for that area.

The 112 metropolitan surveys might be said to present a paradox concerning metropolitan problems and solutions. According to the survey reports, the metropolitan areas are suffering from essentially the same common core set of governmental problems. Yet the reports recommend a wide variety of tailor-made solutions, rather than a single pattern suitable for all metropolitan communities. The surveys indicate that divergent political, social, economic and physical characteristics of the metropolitan communities require different strategies for achieving similar goals.[6]

An illustration of this fact is the strong hostility engendered in the suburbs by Milwaukee's annexation policy since World War II. As a result, any policy decisions within the County at the present day—and in the years to come—will have to take into account the strength of this animosity built up over time.

Evolutionary treatment complements quite effectively the one-year snapshot picture given by the cross-sectional type of study. Perhaps it is not unlike a doctor diagnosing a patient: he wants to know the present state of health as well as the past medical history. Similarly, to prescribe medication, treatments, and cures for metropolitan diseases, it is useful to know not only today's symptoms but also the area's history.

An historical study also complements the aggregative or macro studies that simultaneously examine large numbers of metropolitan areas.[7] Again, it is not a question of one taking the place of the other. Rather, each of these two approaches

6. Government Affairs Foundation, Inc., *Metropolitan Surveys: A Digest* (Chicago, Public Administration Service, 1958), p. 23.

7. Examples of such studies would be Harvey E. Brazer, *City Expenditures in the United States* (New York: National Bureau of Economic Research, 1959); Amos H. Hawley, "Metropolitan Population and Municipal Government Expenditures in Central Cities," *Journal of Social Issues* 7 (1951):100–108; Stanley Scott and Edward L. Feder, *Factors Associated with Variations in Municipal Expenditure Levels* (Berkeley: University of California Press, 1957); Alan K. Campbell and Seymour Sacks, *Metropolitan America* (New York: The Free Press, 1967).

can contribute information because of the particular view-point from which it looks at the problem. The aggregative studies, by deliberately blurring individual characteristics of this or that metropolitan area, can better examine the broad lines, the general features. The value of such an approach is clear for national policy-making, for national long-range planning, and for seeing the universal elements common to all metropolitan areas. However, this rubbing out of detail, this conscious glossing over the individuating elements of a particular area, obviously hides much reality. One who is interested in aiding a specific metropolitan area toward a possible solution of its difficulties finds a picture without de-tails a poor guide to action.

Methodology

Apart from the fact that this is a financial study and an historical study, there are some definitions and procedures to be mentioned. The term "metropolitan" is not used here according to the definition of Standard Metropolitan Statisti-cal Areas [SMSA]. That use of the term would include, in 1970, Milwaukee County (with its 19 localities) as well as Ozaukee County, Washington County, and Waukesha County (with their 38 localities). Instead, the study is confined to Milwaukee County. The reasons are many and cogent; among them are the following: (1) this is an historical study covering the last five decades; by no definition, were the other counties part of the Milwaukee Metropolitan Area 40 or 50 years ago; (2) as late as 1960, Ozaukee County and Washington County were not part of the Milwaukee SMSA; (3) the counties per-form different services for their citizens and this would require numerous qualifications to later figures; (4) the revenue-ex-penditure patterns of the counties are notably different (e.g., in 1960 for county purposes Milwaukee collected about $33 per capita in property taxes and Waukesha collected only $4 per capita); (5) even in 1967 the part of the total SMSA outside of Milwaukee County was rather minor (19 percent of the population and a far smaller percentage of local taxes, expenditures, etc.); (6) the inclusion of the other counties would so load the study with figures that it would be necessary radically to reduce the detailed treatment of the Milwaukee County localities. Needless to say, a larger number of localities in the universe would be welcome for statistical purposes, but the above reasons clearly make it necessary to rule out this desirable feature.

Limitation of the study to the localities within Milwaukee County has profound influence on the central hypothesis. That is, since the area is defined in terms of fixed geographical boundaries (rather than in terms of some flexible norm), it is certainly to be expected that the localities will draw closer to one another in their fiscal personalities as they also draw closer to one another in their process of urbanization. If the constantly expanding SMSA were taken as the object of inquiry (thereby always adding in more rural communities), a trend toward growing homogeneity would be less likely to appear. But with the present definition, a trend toward uniformity can be more logically postulated.

The phrase "local government," as used in this work, will refer to cities, villages, and towns. The taxes and expenditures of school districts will all be apportioned to the above units. County finances are not dealt with specifically, but county tax rates are included in the property rates of the individual localities. The number of local units within the county has fluctuated between 17 and 20 during the period of investigation. At present there are 19.

The basic study covers the 50-year period from 1920 to 1970. The five decades were divided up into 17 time periods. For the first 30 years information was collected at five-year intervals, and then for the last 20 years—that is, the decades of the 1950s and 1960s—every two years. Closer examination during the later years seemed to be required both for deeper comprehension and for sounder prediction.

3 The History

THE MUNICIPALITIES of Milwaukee County fall naturally into four chronological groupings. The local units are classified by the period in which they were established. Fiscal evolution is the main focus; classifying by age highlights the fiscal implications.

A few introductory words about the political and administrative arrangement of government in Wisconsin will be useful. The state is divided into 72 counties, and the counties in turn are divided into towns. The words "town" and "township" are often used interchangeably, even though there are, strictly speaking, no townships in Wisconsin. The towns are laid out in 36-square-mile plots insofar as topography permits. Both the county and the town are the local administrative arms of the state government.

The terms "annexation," "incorporation," "consolidation" will be used quite frequently. Annexation involves taking over a part of an unincorporated locality (a town in Wisconsin) by an incorporated locality (a city or village in Wisconsin). A town may never annex, nor may a part of a city or village be annexed. The major criteria for valid annexation are contiguity of the two areas in question, prior posting of the area to be annexed, signing of a petition for annexation, and a favorable vote by a majority of electors and one-half the owners of real estate in the area to be annexed. Consolidation is annexation on a grand scale. That is, it is the union of an entire town with a neighboring incorporated locality,

19

whereby the town loses its identity. Consolidation can also join two incorporated localities. Incorporation is the act whereby an entire town, or part of a town, petitions the state legislature for village or city status. Such an area must have certain urban characteristics, and, by being incorporated, acquires more powers, independence, and responsibilities—and (an important consideration in Milwaukee County) after incorporation, annexation by another locality becomes impossible.

Group I Communities

The first group of localities is composed of the central city of Milwaukee and the original seven towns of Milwaukee County. They are pictured in Fig. 1 as they were in 1846.

In Milwaukee County the original towns shrank and dis-

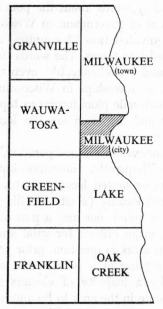

University of Wisconsin Cartographic Laboratory

FIG. 1 Milwaukee County in 1846.

appeared in a variety of ways. Some of them incorporated into cities. Some of them were reduced in size by the incorporation of a part of the town area. Some of them were whittled away by annexation from neighboring cities and villages. This gradual disintegration of towns in Milwaukee County resulted by 1960 in the complete disappearance of unincorporated territory. The phasing out of towns in Milwaukee County was strongly influenced by financial factors.

The central city of Milwaukee began as a village in 1836 and received its city charter ten years later. The little city on the banks of the Milwaukee River and Lake Michigan grew steadily, especially as a result of large German immigration, until in 1900 it had 286,000 people living within city limits of 22 square miles.

During the 1800s Milwaukee experienced in advance some of the patterns that would characterize the whole county during the period of this study (1920–1970). For example, the rivalry among the wards of the city was a prelude to a later animosity between the city of Milwaukee and its suburbs. Also, in the matter of indebtedness, present-day Milwaukee doesn't know what heavy debt is compared with 1858, for at that time the total indebtedness of $2,500,000 was out of all proportion with $6,000,000 of assessed valuation in the young city.[1] Likewise, the lack of cooperation between the city and the state legislature in this century was previewed better than a hundred years ago. Finally, even the problem of transportation is not an entirely new development of our automobile day, but was a growing concern of the city in the last century. For example, a correspondent of the *Milwaukee Daily Journal* on September 12, 1891, thanked divine providence for providing electricity as a mode of transportation. He wrote: "Now a person can make a date with the reasonable certainty of getting there in time. But when the old mu-ly, mu-ly, mu-ly jog was in force, parents living on the east side would kiss their little ones with tender solicitude before starting out for the west, and vice versa, for like men

1. Bayrd Still, *Milwaukee: The History of a City* (Madison: The State Historical Society of Wisconsin, 1948), p. 145.

who go out in ships, the length of their absence was uncertain."[2]

Another development significant for a fiscal analysis was the gradual changeover of the city of Milwaukee from a trading center to an industrial and manufacturing center. A large part of this increase in manufacturing was in heavy machinery, a characteristic of Milwaukee today.

The local press has made much of Milwaukee's annexation policy, especially since World War II. The city did, indeed, add a great deal of land to its original borders. During the 50 years of this study, Milwaukee more than tripled its land area. Over the past 15 years, while its area increased by over 40 percent, the central city has, nonetheless, been declining in total population. The newspaper image of powerful Milwaukee greedily gobbling up the helpless suburbs is quite misleading. The suburbs were also doing their share of annexing. Of the 15 municipalities that were already incorporated while "annexable" land was still available, 11 of them did, as a matter of fact, add to their area by annexation. Hence, while Milwaukee was receiving the publicity, nearly all the municipalities were receiving the land.

Of the seven original towns in Milwaukee County, there were, as of 1970, four localities which still bore the names of the former towns. These are Franklin, Oak Creek, Greenfield, and Wauwatosa, all of them now cities. But even these have different boundary lines from their town days.

Franklin is one of the least urbanized localities in Milwaukee County. The only change in Franklin's area from its original 36 square miles was the loss of two square miles through the incorporation of Greendale in 1938. Throughout its history, Franklin has undergone little population growth. As late as 1954, it could be stated that "farms in the town of Franklin constitute 88 percent of the area and 36 percent of the equalized assessed valuation."[3] And yet, in spite of this strongly rural character, Franklin was incorporated as a city

2. Quoted ibid., p. 370.

3. *Citizens Governmental Research Bureau Bulletin* 42, no. 14 (August 6, 1954), p. 1 [cited hereafter as *CGRB Bulletin*].

just two years later. This strange development was made possible by a legislative enactment to be discussed shortly.

Like Franklin, Oak Creek had few boundary changes in
its history from the days in 1840 when it was laid out with
34 square miles. Its only significant loss of area was the incorporation of South Milwaukee as a village in 1892, leaving
Oak Creek with its present 28.5 square miles.

Wisconsin statutes used to insist that certain urban characteristics had to exist before an area could be incorporated.
The key requirement was that a town have a population density of 400 people per square mile (Wisconsin Statutes, Sections 61.01 and 62.06). Largely at the instigation of Oak
Creek, a law was passed in the Wisconsin Legislature in 1955
removing the density requirement. This law, known as the
"Oak Creek Law," raised a great furor in Milwaukee County.
It was challenged in the courts but ruled valid. As a result,
even though it had only about 240 people per square mile,
Oak Creek incorporated itself as a fourth-class city a few
months after the law was passed.

Oak Creek had a very definite reason for wanting the pas-
sage of this law. During the early 1950s the Wisconsin Electric
Power Company started the construction of a $300,000,000
power plant within the boundaries of Oak Creek. To understand the full import of this power plant to Oak Creek it
is necessary to know something about the Wisconsin system
of sharing utility taxes.

The state department of taxation determines the full market value
(equalized assessed valuation) of electric power companies. The
property tax to be paid by the electric power company equals the
property value multiplied by the equalized property tax rate
throughout Wisconsin. The state retains fifteen percent of the
property taxes which it collects from electric power companies,
gives twenty percent to the county, and sixty-five percent to the
towns, cities, and villages "in or through which business of such
company was carried on and operated in proportion, as near as
may be, to the property located and the business transacted within
each such town, city and village." (Chapter 76.28 (1) 1953 Wisconsin Statutes.) The Wisconsin Supreme Court has stated that in

computing the amount of the tax collections to be distributed to each locality the value of the property located within the town, city or village must count the same as the annual electric sales in each community.[4]

The last sentence of this quotation explains the eagerness of Oak Creek to become a city. For, by incorporating as a city, Oak Creek killed the possibility of any neighboring village or city annexing part of its territory, especially the part with the power plant. The dramatic move paid off handsomely. In 1950, Oak Creek received $6,000 in utility revenue from the state; 20 years later it received $2,964,000.

The former town of Lake had a certain kinship with Oak Creek, for one of the town's main sources of revenue was the large Lakeside utility plant situated within its borders. However, in 1951 St. Francis incorporated itself as a new city and drew its borders around the Lakeside Power Plant. Lake, finding its property tax rates rising rapidly, felt compelled to consolidate with the city of Milwaukee. And so, after 1954, the town of Lake ceased to exist.

The town of Milwaukee has spawned more incorporated localities than any of the other towns in Milwaukee County. In addition to the area that went into the original city of Milwaukee, the town of Milwaukee gave birth to six other present-day municipalities. Originally, the town was 26 square miles in area. The incorporation of Whitefish Bay, Shorewood, Fox Point, and River Hills, plus some other chipping away by annexation, cut this area in half by 1950. Then the city of Glendale incorporated around the rich industrial section in the southern part of the town of Milwaukee in 1950. Although the new city took over only 27 percent of the town's area, it acquired 70 percent of the town's assessed valuation. From that time on, it was a rapid process of disintegration (including the incorporation of Bayside in 1953) until the town of Milwaukee completely disappeared in 1955.

The development of Greenfield is perhaps a more typical example of urbanization in a town area close to a large city.

4. Ibid., no. 15 (September 25, 1954), p. e.

Annexations and incorporations reduced the original 36 square miles to 26 by 1940, and to 13 by 1957. In that year the town incorporated itself as the city of Greenfield. In the fiscal and demographic data that follow, Greenfield, Franklin, and Oak Creek will each be treated as the same locality from 1920 to 1970. For, even though all three of these had area changes—in the case of Greenfield, very significant changes—and though all three of them were once towns and are now incorporated areas, yet there is sufficient continuity from their town days to city days to warrant treating each of them as a single locality over time.

It is interesting to note that during the present century, while the area of Greenfield was gradually being chipped away by annexation and incorporation, its population continued to grow within the diminishing area. In fact, one student of towns in Milwaukee County has concluded that towns with the greatest population growth are the ones most subject to area loss, whether by annexation, consolidation, or incorporation.[5] Greenfield was not "prudent" enough to zone out the less productive kind of land users in the way other Milwaukee suburbs did. As a result, the following comment was made in 1956:

Because of the influx of low-income and middle-income families, the area [Greenfield] has elementary school problems and a serious high school problem. Tax levies in some of the school districts have more than tripled in the short span of just five years; some of the districts are approaching the limit of their borrowing capacity and more children—and still more children—are headed for the Greenfield schools. The fact is—Greenfield is learning today what the Engelburg [School] District in Granville learned two years ago— that a $12,000 or a $15,000, or even a $20,000 home does not produce enough in tax revenue to pay for keeping a single child in the elementary school. It is learning that a single subdivision of 100 homes can swamp a school and force an addition to an existing school or construction of a new school.[6]

5. Kathleen Kepner, "Town Government in the Milwaukee Metropolitan Area" (M.A. thesis, University of Wisconsin, 1955), p. 5.
6. Joseph R. Lamping, "Fragmentation," Mimeographed (Milwaukee: Milwaukee Department of Community Development, 1956), p. 12.

A paradox appears in the disappearance of the county's other two original towns, Wauwatosa and Granville. For the six years prior to 1954 the residents of neither town had paid any town taxes; yet, over the next two years those same residents willingly voted to be annexed by a number of neighboring muncipalities. This sounds strange. The explanation in both cases appears to be strikingly similar. Each foresaw the need for an enormous increase in local services (especially capital outlays) and the best way to get them without bearing the whole cost themselves was to agree to be annexed. Thus, for example, it was noted in 1954 that: "A recent study estimates that capital improvements required by the present town area of Wauwatosa during the next ten years will total $23,545,000 for sewers, water mains, streets, sidewalks, a library branch, playgrounds, and schools."[7] One year later the townspeople chose to be annexed by the cities of Wauwatosa, Milwaukee, and West Allis. The town of Granville followed a similar path, for similar reasons.

In the case of the central city and the original seven towns of Milwaukee County, it hardly seems an exaggeration to say that fiscal factors strongly influenced their evolution.

Group II Communities

This second category includes seven localities that came into being around the turn of the century. The purpose of grouping localities by their date of incorporation is not so much for the sake of historical neatness but because the age of a locality has a distinctive influence on its financial development.

Many of the older suburbs were developed in a period of low birth rates. They always had smaller percentages of children of school age in the population than areas built more recently, and consequently a large tax base per school child. Also, in the older suburbs, the construction was more often on an individual basis. There were less of the mass production of new homes than is now

7. *CGRB Bulletin* 42, no. 11 (June 28, 1954), p. 1.

the practice. Hence, the growth was gradual. These different conditions permitted older suburbs to go through periods of growth without high taxes.[8]

Four municipalities in Group II have much in common, even beyond the fact that they were all incorporated between 1892 and 1906. Each of the four grew up around its own industrial base—not as a sleeping or shopping appendage of the central city. Each of them developed as a balanced locality, that is, with a mixture of industrial property, commercial property, and residential property. Thus they all had originally—and continue to have today—more economic justification for being independent municipalities than the county's 13 bedroom communities. In this respect, it should be noted that the four of them were established during the pre-automobile era at a sufficient distance from Milwaukee so that they simply had to be self-sufficient; that is, they had to have their own employment opportunities, homes for their workers, shopping, recreational and cultural facilities, water, sewer, and school systems, etc. This kind of self-containment is found in the residential suburbs. And, finally, just as these four localities resemble the central city so much in their economic mix and their economic independence, so, too (with the exception of West Milwaukee), they resemble the central city in their present fiscal difficulties. The four are South Milwaukee, Cudahy, West Allis, and West Milwaukee.

South Milwaukee was originally an unincorporated community, made up of a few mills, inns, a store, a school, a church, some homes—all clustered around the place where the stream Oak Creek empties into Lake Michigan. A real estate boom began in 1890 during which eight new manufacturing plants and over 50 businesses were opened there. The village of South Milwaukee was then incorporated in 1892; five years later it became a city. The commercial and industrial beginnings of South Milwaukee have characterized it right through its 80-year history.

The very name of Cudahy gives a strong hint of the origin

8. Lamping, "Fragmentation," p. 8.

of this city. The Cudahy Brothers Meat Packing Plant was first located in the city of Milwaukee. There was talk in the late 1800s of a city ordinance that would bear heavily on meat packing plants, and this induced the Cudahy Brothers to move their plant in 1892 some eight miles south of the Milwaukee business district into the town of Lake. When the packing plant was built there, it was just an open area. The village of Cudahy was incorporated in 1895, and 11 years later it achieved the status of a city. Just as Cudahy depended for its beginnings on an industry, so has its growth and development been closely associated with the growth of its three largest industries. In addition to the Cudahy meat packing firm, the other two large industries are the Ladish Drop Forge Company, and the George J. Meyer Manufacturing Company. Even in 1970, close to 60 percent of Cudahy's equalized property value was in the manufacturing and mercantile categories.

If the beginnings of Cudahy can largely be explained in terms of a single firm, then similarly the establishment and development of West Allis can be explained in terms of the Allis-Chalmers Company. In 1901 the Edward P. Allis Company, a machinery manufacturing firm on the south side of Milwaukee, decided to move out in the country to have more area for expansion, to be near railroad transportation facilities, and to enable its workers to live nearby. This led to a real estate boom in the area involving both industrial and residential growth. The village was incorporated in 1902, just a year after the Allis Company moved out there, and four years later it became a city.

The original area of the city was three square miles, and this stayed pretty much the same until 1950, but its population had grown to 43,000 people. Within the next ten years that figure jumped to 68,000. This great growth during the 1950s is to be explained not in terms of new people moving into the original boundaries of West Allis, but rather in terms of the large areas that it annexed during this period. With 71,723 residents in 1970, West Allis is the fourth largest city in the state of Wisconsin. Thus, this "suburb" of Milwaukee is much larger than many of Wisconsin's "central cities."

If West Allis can be classified as an industrial suburb, then West Milwaukee would have to be termed a super-industrial suburb. This little village was incorporated in 1906, some years after the Harnischfeger Corporation had been established there. Its area was then but 0.7 of a square mile, and even today it is just over 1 square mile. West Milwaukee has not grown much in population over the past 40 years for the simple reason that most of its land area is zoned industrial. In 1970, it had $43,357 in equalized property valuation per capita, whereas the county average for that year was $8,171 per capita. Back in 1935, the first time that such figures are capable of being calculated, we find that West Milwaukee had 40 percent of its total property in residential property; this dropped to 29 percent in 1950, and to 10 percent in 1970. The other 90 percent was in mercantile and manufacturing property, almost entirely the latter.

In 1960, there were approximately 13,000 persons employed in the firms of West Milwaukee.[9] The significance of this figure lies in the fact that the total resident population of the village (men, women, and children) was only 5,043 in that same year. It is easy to see the effect of this high industrial concentration on the governmental finances of West Milwaukee. Even though it could draw heavily on its industrial base for property taxes, because of the large amount of corporate income taxes returned to it by the state, the village is almost embarrassed by its riches and, as a result, makes little use of its industrial property base. West Milwaukee is the fourth suburb encountered thus far with a decidedly industrial complexion. Yet, to keep this fact in perspective, it should be recalled that even as late as 1959 the central city still had about 90 percent of all manufacturing plants in the county and about 80 percent of all employees engaged in manufacturing within the county.

Wauwatosa was incorporated in 1892 with a population of 1,150 people living in an area of three square miles. According to the 1970 census, those three square miles have since grown to 13, and those 1,150 people have grown to 58,676.

9. *CGRB Bulletin* 44, no. 6 (March 14, 1956), p. 2.

The city is a residential suburb with an unusually high level of home ownership. Most Wauwatosans work in the neighboring cities of West Allis and Milwaukee. The level of income has been about one-third above the level of Milwaukee County (which is already high relative to the rest of the state).

Whitefish Bay is one of the many localities formed from the former town of Milwaukee. Situated north of the city of Milwaukee, along Lake Michigan, it used to be a famous recreation area for the people of Milwaukee around the turn of the century. The Pabst Whitefish Bay Resort was built in the late 1800s; it consisted of a hotel, a pavilion, picnic areas, gardens, a beach, etc. Shortly after the incorporation of Whitefish Bay (1892) a financial panic held back the development of the village for quite some time; as late as 1920 there were only 800 residents in the municipality's two square miles. Then, between 1920 and 1930, the population mushroomed to 5,000. This has grown steadily to 17,394 people in 1970, living in the same two square miles. Whitefish Bay is a strictly residential community whose development has proceeded in accordance with a comprehensive zoning ordinance adopted in 1922.

The village of Shorewood lies just north of the city of Milwaukee along Lake Michigan and, therefore, between Milwaukee and Whitefish Bay. In 1900 some land had already been subdivided for sale and the village was incorporated as East Milwaukee; it wasn't until 1917 that the name was changed to Shorewood. The original area of the newly incorporated village was 1.6 square miles and this has stayed the same over the past seventy years. Within this one and a half square miles in 1970 lived 15,576 people— just a shade below the 15,907 people in 1960.

The following quotation indicates some of the factors which make the fiscal development of Group II localities different from those that are to follow:

Cudahy, South Milwaukee, West Allis, and West Milwaukee had industry to help carry the tax load. And factories, big stores, and shops and garages, send no children to school. But they do pay school taxes. As they developed, Shorewood, Whitefish Bay, and Wauwatosa had the benefit of population made up principally of upper-income and big-income families. In the days when these communities were building up, automobile ownership was limited, and an automobile was a virtual necessity for those who took up residence in suburbia. As a result, the communities developed much more slowly than the newer cities and villages, with no sudden impacts on schools or school taxes.[10]

TABLE 1
Municipality Density Rank, 1920-1970

Municipality	1920ᵃ	1930	Density Rank 1940	1950	1960	1970
Cudahy	3	5	6	7	8	6
Milwaukee	1	1	1	1	3	3
Shorewood	6	3	3	2	1	1
S. Milwaukee	7	8	8	8	7	5
Wauwatosa	5	6	5	5	6	7
W. Allis	2	2	2	3	4	4
W. Milwaukee	4	4	4	4	5	8
Whitefish Bay	10	7	7	6	2	2

Source: US Department of Commerce, Bureau of the Census, for both population and land data.
ᵃ In 1920 the towns of Wauwatosa and Lake ranked 8 and 9, respectively, in population density.

One might expect the older communities of Group II (along with the central city) to have higher than average population density. As a matter of fact, the association of age and density holds up with remarkable consistency. As the data in Table 1 show, the eight municipalities that incorporated first have been, with one minor exception, the first eight of all county localities when ranked by population density.

10. Lamping, "Fragmentation," pp. 2–3.

Group III Communities

The two big periods of new incorporations in Milwaukee County were the years around the turn of the century (Group II) and the decade of the 1950s (Group IV). Between these two periods three other localities came into existence. The first of them was Fox Point, incorporated in 1926; the second was River Hills, incorporated in 1930; and the third was Greendale, incorporated in 1938. These three are somewhat intermediate between the slow, gradual development of the communities in Group II and the abrupt, unprepared emergence to be seen in Group IV.

The village of Fox Point is situated north of Whitefish Bay, bordering on Lake Michigan. From the beginning Fox Point has been a residential area with very stringent zoning regulations that prevented any but the wealthy from living there. One effect of these regulations has been to guarantee a high property tax base per person. Secondly, they ruled out the possibility of mass housing subdivisions and thereby ruled out the calamitous effects on school costs subdivisions often cause. And thirdly, in Wisconsin, where a significant part of the state income tax is returned to the locality of residence, the zoning regulations assured Fox Point of a generous check each year from the state treasury.

River Hills was incorporated just four years after Fox Point. Almost everything said about Fox Point can be said with equal truth, plus a little more emphasis, about River Hills. This village has an even higher property valuation per capita; has even more high income residents who bring a very healthy returned income tax from the state; and has even tighter zoning restrictions limiting the size of lot on which one can build. Through the years, River Hills has been first or second in the whole county in its rank of taxable property per capita.

Greendale is most unusual. This village started as a federal government project in the depression days of 1936—one of three experimental, carefully planned suburban communities engineered by Washington. All the property in the villlage belonged to the federal government, which arranged the lay-

out, the development, and the rate of growth in the new
community. There could, therefore, be no meaningful local
property tax rate. The government sold the homes to residents
in 1952, and then in 1953 it sold the village administration
building, shopping center, and the remaining 3.5 square miles
to a private group (Milwaukee Community Development Corporation). The best way to treat Greendale during the period
of its federal ownership is to omit it from the data compila-
tions. In more recent years, however, it has come to take
a normal place among the localities of Milwaukee County.

Group IV Communities

All five of the localities in this classification were incorporated between 1950 and 1955. The first is Glendale. In the
southern part of the town of Milwaukee in the late 1940s
was a solidly established industrial complex. The city of Milwaukee was naturally interested in adding this area to its
boundaries. With such a threat before them, the citizens in
this section of the town banded together and formed a small
industrial suburb in 1950, calling it Glendale. To this day,
the community has close to 60 percent of its property values
in business categories. An industrial suburb benefits in two
ways as far as local governmental revenue is concerned: first,
the industrial property itself adds to the base for the general
property tax (without sending children to the schools); and
secondly, a large percentage of the corporate income tax
levied by the state is returned to the locality in which the
corporation is located.

Once known as Deer Creek, St. Francis is a small suburb
carved out of the town of Lake shortly before that town's
consolidation with Milwaukee. As noted earlier, this city was
incorporated around the large Lakeside utility plant to prevent the property tax bonanza from being annexed by the
city of Milwaukee. The huge new electric utility plant in
Oak Creek has greatly reduced the windfall value of the older
utility plant to the city of St. Francis.

Although not incorporated until 1952, Hales Corners has.

a long history as a community. It was a crossroads and trading center for the surrounding rural area in the last century. It became the location of a well-known monthly fair for which farmers and others came from many miles around. Hales Corners was a rather well-developed part of the town of Greenfield; in the early 1950s, the rest of the town began to demand the kind of urbanized services which Hales Corners residents had already put in and paid for. Having taxed themselves once for their own capital improvements, the residents were reluctant to tax themselves again to provide similar improvements for the rest of the town. So they incorporated their little section (six square miles) to separate themselves fiscally from the rest of the town.

If the grouping of localities were by type rather than by age, Bayside would be included with Fox Point and River Hills; it is quite close to them in most respects. Although Bayside was incorporated many years later, it follows these other two in its reasons for incorporation, in its manner of development, in its source of revenue, and in the type of residents that it has. The following description of Bayside, even though it is 15 years old, says practically all that is to be said for the purpose of this background:

> The village of Bayside is a residential community of fine homes and high income families. The percentage of families with an annual income in excess of $7,000 is four times that of Milwaukee County as a whole. New construction is limited to single family dwellings conforming to the design and value of existing residences. The average value of homes in the village exceeds $25,000, exclusive of land costs. Industrial and commercial developments are prohibited by village zoning regulations.[11]

Brown Deer was incorporated in 1955 with four square miles taken from the town of Granville. There were about 2,000 people living there at that time. Shortly after it incorporated, Brown Deer attempted to annex the rest of the town of Granville (some 20 square miles). While this attempt was going on, the city of Milwaukee obtained a favorable vote

11. *CGRB Bulletin* 44, no. 4 (February 21, 1956), pp. 1, 3.

from Granville residents to annex all the remaining area of
the town to the city. The conflicting claims of Brown Deer
and Milwaukee went to court in 1957. It wasn't until April
3, 1962, that the Wisconsin Supreme Court finally settled the
issue, largely in favor of Milwaukee. In the intervening years,
each of the litigants was administering parcels temporarily
assigned to it by lower courts. Later data on population, expenditures, property values, etc., will reflect this temporary
arrangement.

It is clear how different this fourth group is from the earlier
localities. "Since 1950 almost 3/4 of the county, which was
previously unincorporated rural hinterland, has been incorporated or absorbed by annexation or consolidation to existing
municipalities. The present pattern is not actually a result
of normal historical development, but of the fusion of the
traditional pattern with large relatively undeveloped areas
and with a new suburban oriented philosophy of large lot,
high income, and low density residential development."[12]

Three points emerge from the preceding overview. For one
thing, political and economic decisions were frequently influenced by considerations of fiscal self-interest (in the sense
of public or governmental finance). It would, of course, be
an exaggeration to say that this fiscal factor supplies the magic
key which opens up and explains the whole evolution of Milwaukee County.

Secondly, this historical sketch brings out the great social
and economic interdependence of the localities in Milwaukee
County. To have five municipalities side by side with nothing
in them but residences (Milwaukee County's northeast section) would be impossible if they were cut off from a metropolitan area, that is, cut off from other localities where these
people can earn a living. Similarly, to have 13,000 people
engaged in manufacturing in a village of 5,000 residents
(West Milwaukee) would be impossible outside of a metro-

12. Metropolitan Study Commission, *An Analysis of Land Use and
Zoning in Milwaukee County, Wisconsin* (Milwaukee: MSC, 1959),
p. 18.

politan area. "The metropolitan area serves as a combination assembly line and market place where persons and goods are interchanged in the process of satisfying human wants. Individuals who live in one community—work in another—to manufacture products for sale in a third—to persons who reside in still a fourth locality. The specific roles played by the different individuals and communities are diversified, but the total process is one of economic unity."[13]

Thirdly, and perhaps more important, the historical background makes it clear how closely related are the two points just mentioned. That is the economic unity of the metropolitan area which gives rise to the interdependence of the localities similarly gives rise to their financial advantage (or disadvantage) relative to one another. Thus, the very thing that makes the metropolitan area possible (its economic unity) results in some parts of the area securing benefit at the expense of other parts. Or, to put it another way, the basic unity is the source of the area's disunity; the economic oneness of the whole is being used for economic advantage of the parts; the factor which by economic logic should pull them all together is being used to divide them.[14]

13. James A. Norton, *Prologue to Progress* (Cleveland: Cleveland Metropolitan Services Commission, 1959), pp. 11–12.
14. Robert C. Wood, *Metropolis Against Itself* (New York: Committee for Economic Development, 1959), p. 33.

4 Property Tax Base

THE PROPERTY tax provides about 85 percent of locally raised taxes. This dependence on the property tax by local government seems unfortunate—not only because tangible property bears but a tenuous relationship to wealth and income, but also because such a dependence leaves so little flexibility for local government. The problem of inflexibility has been intensified in the Milwaukee area by the action of the Wisconsin Legislature, which enacted in 1947 a statute forbidding any local income tax within the state.[1] One of the main reasons offered for this legislation was the fear on the part of the state government that local income taxes would inhibit future expansion of the state income tax.[2] If the same reasoning be applied, the enactment of a state sales tax in 1961 would seem to also rule out this source of revenue for local governments. The result for the Milwaukee area is that the present dependence on property tax as a source of local revenue is likely to continue.

In Wisconsin only tangible property is taxable. In fact, the state income tax was enacted in 1911 to compensate for the revenue lost by removal of intangible property from the tax

1. Section 66.70 of the Wisconsin Statutes reads: "No county, city, village, town or other unit of government authorized to levy taxes shall assess, levy, or collect any tax on income, or measured by income, and any such tax so levied or assessed is void."

2. William D. Knight, *Wisconsin Legislative Council, 1950 Report: Taxation* (Madison: State Legislature, 1950), p. 213.

rolls in that year. Assessments are carried out by locally appointed or elected officials (often on a part-time basis). In addition to the local property assessment, there is a "reassessment" of all property by state officials. Although the local assessment is the basis of the local tax rate, the valuation supplied on the state level (called "full value" or "equalized value") is used for county tax rates, and for certain state-levied property taxes (e.g., those on railroads, public utilities, etc.). Obviously, these equalized values are also of great value to the researcher, for they offer a reliable basis of comparison among localities within the state;[3] this is all the more welcome in view of the well-deserved reputation the Wisconsin equalization process has won.[4] In the discussion which follows, only equalized values and equalized tax rates will be used. Table 2 lists in per capita terms the total equalized property values (real and personal) for each locality over the past ten years.[5]

One notable feature of property values over the entire 50 years is the regularity with which all municipalities follow general trends; the variations and oscillations of the individual municipalities are seen to occur along the trend line of the group. Thus, nearly all of the municipalities grew in per capita property valuation through the 1920s. Then came the depression of the 1930s; every single locality of the area

3. Harvey E. Brazer, *City Expenditures in the United States* (New York: National Bureau of Economic Research, 1959), p. 24. Brazer regrets that he is unable to use property values in his study of city expenditures because of this comparability problem.

4. Clara Penniman, "Property Tax Equalization in Wisconsin," *National Tax Journal* 14 (June 1961):182–89.

5. Similar data for the years 1920–60 can be found in Donald J. Curran, "The Financial Evolution of the Milwaukee Metropolitan Area" (Ph.D. Diss.; University of Wisconsin, 1963). Although the data for earlier decades are crucial for the historical approach of this study, their actual reproduction here is not at all crucial. The basic messages of the earlier figures are discussed herein; the tables showing the tests of the central hypotheses are all given in full; and the "feel" for the magnitudes involved is provided in the tables covering the past ten years, e.g., Table 2.

TABLE 2
Per Capita Equalized Property Valuations For
Municipalities of Milwaukee County, 1960–1970

	1960	1962	1964	1966	1968	1970
Milwaukee	$ 5,075	$ 5,233	$ 5,348	$ 5,678	$ 6,210	$ 7,010
Bayside	9,890	10,430	10,398	11,046	11,828	13,210
Brown Deer	5,385	4,305	4,463	5,509	7,056	8,977
Cudahy	6,721	7,139	7,559	8,508	8,945	9,755
Fox Point	9,974	10,288	10,387	11,259	11,862	13,337
Franklin	4,270	4,271	4,273	4,668	5,103	6,160
Glendale	13,831	14,648	15,136	16,460	17,844	19,617
Greendale	4,359	4,868	4,823	5,298	6,102	8,247
Greenfield	4,571	4,606	4,612	5,030	5,722	7,257
Hales Corners	6,475	6,574	6,534	6,673	7,430	8,795
Oak Creek	6,620	7,175	8,087	8,694	11,299	12,205
River Hills	14,922	15,557	15,790	16,543	16,874	19,165
St. Francis	3,471	3,845	4,090	4,314	4,779	5,419
Shorewood	5,882	6,000	6,245	6,922	7,686	8,917
S. Milwaukee	5,279	5,560	5,713	5,919	6,437	7,176
Wauwatosa	7,080	7,591	8,017	9,025	10,402	12,111
W. Allis	6,866	6,908	7,395	7,856	8,922	10,453
W. Milwaukee	27,843	29,954	30,579	34,440	37,838	43,357
Whitefish Bay	6,840	6,942	7,104	7,692	8,261	9,808
Suburbs Only	6,990	7,228	7,527	8,197	9,196	10,643
Entire County	5,620	5,815	5,999	6,448	7,143	8,171

Source: State of Wisconsin, Office of Tax Commission, Assessors of Incomes Statistical Report of Property Valuations for the County of Milwaukee for respective years.

suffered a drop in per capita property value between 1930 and 1935. This dramatic fall-off in tax base was, as will be noted later, matched by an equally dramatic rise in tax rates in the same five-year period. Better than two-thirds of the localities show recovery during the second half of the 1930s after the bottom had been hit in 1932–34; the recovery continued during the war years. And, finally, the influence of the postwar prosperity is mirrored in a continuous and notable rise in per capita valuation for nearly all localities in all time periods from 1945 to 1970. An appreciable part of this great rise in property values in recent years is, of course, the result of inflation.

With these general remarks as background, the central question can be posed: is there a trend toward greater or less uniformity in property tax resources within Milwaukee County over these 50 years? This raises the problem of a satisfactory test of variation. Clearly, some measure is desired which allows for the changing level of per capita figures over time. The coefficient of quartile variation (the formula for this coefficient is: $V_q = Q3 - Q1/Q3 + Q1 \cdot 100$) has been chosen as the most informative for present purposes. Admittedly, this has the following drawbacks: (a) it tells nothing about the extent to which a locality or two at either extreme may depart from the quartile figure; (b) occasionally it permits a single locality to swing the coefficient unduly because of the small number of municipalities within the county; and (c) it does not measure whether any observable changes are significant or not. As to (a), the absence of this kind of information is not harmful. Our desire is to know the general trends or movements of the whole group over time; the degree to which one or two members depart from that group is relatively unimportant. In fact, one reason for choosing the quartile coefficient over the other common measure of variation (the standard deviation divided by the means) is the fact that it is far less sensitive to the extremely wide departure of one or two members. For present purposes, such sensitivity would be quite misleading. As to (b), the small number in the universe certainly suggests caution in interpreting results. And where a single locality has disproportionate influence on the coefficient, comment will be made on it. As to (c), this is a reminder to recognize the results for what they are—suggestive hints and little more. In spite of these drawbacks, this measure assuredly gives a more reliable picture than simple observation.

Table 3 lists the coefficient of quartile variation for the municipal property values over 50 years. An increase in the coefficient of variation would suggest an increase in spread

TABLE 3
Coefficients of Quartile Variation in
Per Capita Property Values for
Municipalities of Milwaukee County,
1920-1970

1920–1945		1950–1970	
Year	Coefficient	Year	Coefficient
1920	33.1	1950	39.0
1925	31.6	1952	30.8
1930	39.3	1954	31.5
1935	42.8	1956	35.1
1940	35.5	1958	33.0
1945	43.3	1960	32.1
		1962	35.8
		1964	36.6
		1966	33.4
		1968	31.1
		1970	23.6

Sources: data in Table 2; Donald J. Curran, "The Financial Evolution of the Milwaukee Metropolitan Area" (Ph.D. Diss., University of Wisconsin, 1963), pp. 80–81.

and hence a lessening of homogeneity. The significance of this table is that there is no indication of increasing or of decreasing homogeneity in property values among these municipalities from 1920 to 1970. There are numerous other points of interest in the table, but these should not distract attention from the basic fact that there appears to be roughly the same amount of variation in fiscal resources (in terms of taxable property) throughout the entire period. The numerous jumps in the coefficient values all during the 50 years keep coming back close to the average variation; thus, it would seem improper to read a new trend into the years since 1964.

To say that there is no indication of changes in uniformity over time is a far cry, however, from saying that the municipalities are similar to one another in per capita property values. The differences are striking. This is true regardless of the time period chosen. In 1970, for example, West Milwaukee had eight times as much taxable property per capita as St. Francis. It may be overstating the case to compare an industrial suburb like West Milwaukee with its neighbors. Take River Hills, then, with 95 per cent of its property in the residential category. In 1935 River Hills had six times as much property per person as Cudahy and South Milwaukee, neither of which could be called rural or underdeveloped. Or, perhaps one might expect to find uniformity between two municipalities with land uses that are well balanced among residential, mercantile, and manufacturing. Milwaukee (with 44 percent of its total property classified as residential in 1970) and Glendale (with 43 percent so classified) provide a good illustration. One looks in vain, however, for uniformity; for the past 15 years Glendale regularly had about three times as much taxable property per capita as the city of Milwaukee.

The finding of no growth in homogeneity is somewhat similar to what Jesse Burkhead found in the Cleveland area, where he had the benefit of a much larger sample, but the drawback of only two time periods in some cases, three in others.[6] He found some growing similarity in the per capita property values of cities and villages, but a lessening of similarity among school districts. Where growth in homogeneity existed, it occurred between 1940 and 1950; between 1950 and 1956 it leveled off.

Given the main conclusion above, Table 3 still reveals interesting movements in the coefficients of variation over time. Between 1925 and 1930, for example, the rather sharp departure from uniformity is attributable to the fact that richer localities (i.e., the top quartile in property valuation) grew in wealth during the prosperity of the late 1920s much faster than the other three quartiles. Between 1935 and 1940, on the other hand, the bottom part of the distribution moved

6. Jesse Burkhead, "Uniformity in Governmental Expenditures and Resources in a Metropolitan Area: Cuyahoga County," *National Tax Journal* 14 (December 1961):337–48.

up from the depths of the depression much more than the rest, resulting in a move toward increased homogeneity of resources. The notable lessening of uniformity between 1940 and 1945 results from the fact that two highly industrialized localities increased their property tax base much more than the rest, pushing the bottom of the top quartile up to an impressive degree. The great growth in property values of these two manufacturing communities was associated with war production.

The second part of the major hypothesis deals with the question of greater or less homogeneity as between the central city and its suburbs taken as a group. Two time periods stand out: (1) 1920–40, during which the central city and suburbs moved independently but managed to stay near each other; and (2) 1940–70, during which they both manifested growth, but at rates which moved them further and further apart. Thus, the suburbs grew at a rate of 495 percent in the last 30 years, while the central city grew at a rate of only 371 percent—boosting the per capita dollar difference between them from $297 in 1940 to $3,633 in 1970. Further, even if we take the whole 50-year period, the rate of suburban growth is faster than Milwaukee's. Therefore, we are compelled to conclude that there is some tendency away from homogeneity between the central city and its suburbs in terms of per capita property valuation. Or, to put it another way, the city of Milwaukee has had a property tax base below the suburban average for 50 years, and during that time its relatively bad position has been getting progressively worse.

What puts Milwaukee at such a disadvantage compared with its suburbs is its large amount of middle and low income residential property. Thus, to take 1960 as a typical illustration of recent decades, the central city ranked sixth out of the 19 county localities in per capita value of industrial and mercantile property, but it ranked eighteenth out of 19 in residential property per capita. The result of this poverty in residential property was that Milwaukee found itself fifteenth out of 19 in total property per capita. This sobering fact should be kept in mind for the later discussion of zoning and suburban specialization and for what Robert Wood calls "municipal mercantilism."[7]

Table 4 is another way of indicating how the suburbs have been outstripping the central city in their rate of property growth. The dollar amounts underlying the percentages of Table 4 are absolute numbers, not per capita numbers. These

TABLE 4
City of Milwaukee's Share of All Taxable
Property in Milwaukee County, 1920–1970

1920–1945		1950–1970	
Year	Percentage	Year	Percentage
1920	81	1950	68
1925	81	1952	68
1930	78	1954	68
1935	77	1956	68
1940	73	1958	66
1945	69	1960	65
		1962	64
		1964	63
		1966	61
		1968	60
		1970	58

Source: State of Wisconsin, Office of Tax Commission, Assessors of Incomes Statistical Report of Property Valuations for the County of Milwaukee for the given years.

percentages become even more impressive when it is recalled that the city of Milwaukee added greatly to its land area during those 50 years. Its share of county property value dropped from 81 percent to 58 percent during a period when its area grew from 26 square miles to over 90 square miles.

7. Robert C. Wood, *1400 Governments: The Political Economy of the New York Metropolitan Region* (Cambridge, Mass.: Harvard University Press, 1961), pp. 112, 174, et passim.

Is there growing homogeneity between groups differen-
tiated on the basis of their date of incorporation? Are the
newer cities and villages drawing closer financially to the
older ones? This is not an idle question. A town usually incor-
porates because it finds its rural political machinery is no
longer adequate. Thus, under investigation is the rather reasonable expectation that increased "urbanness" (reflected in
the decision to incorporate) leads a locality to grow financially
more like those that are already urban (i.e., long since
incorporated).

The fact that there are at present no unincorporated localities in Milwaukee County does not lessen the forecasting
potential of this question. The Milwaukee Metropolitan Area,
like all others, is constantly spreading out, ever growing new
layers; in 1970 it embraced three other counties besides Milwaukee County. These new layers, or metropolitan fringes,
include unincorporated and newly incorporated municipalities
taking the place of those examined in this study. Thus, if
any trends are discernible within the county, they should
be partly or largely applicable to the new accretions of the
present and future outside the county.

All those localities incorporated before 1920 constitute one
group, and all those incorporated afterward make up the other
group. The first group is therefore constant, and includes the
following eight localities: Cudahy, City of Milwaukee, Shorewood, South Milwaukee, City of Wauwatosa, West Allis, West
Milwaukee, and Whitefish Bay.

The median property tax base (per capita) of each group
was computed for the 17 time periods of the study. The two
points that emerge from tracing these figures are: (1) the
older group has slightly higher property values in every time
period from 1935 onward; and (2) the medians stay consistently close to one another. This may be somewhat contrary
to general expectations. It might be thought that older, more-
established communities would have higher property values
than the less-developed ones during the early years of this
century, with the difference diminishing (or disappearing)
over time. This expectation is partially borne out by the fact

that the poorest communities right on up to the 1950s are almost all unincorporated towns. Yet, this is counterbalanced by the fact that a couple of the towns were rich in property plus the fact that the first new corporations (Fox Point and River Hills) happened to be very wealthy. The result is that in 1940, 1945, and 1950 three of the four wealthiest county municipalities were in the "younger" group, while three of the four poorest municipalities were in this same group.

As new localities were added to the younger group in the 1950s, they pretty well balanced each other out, some being well-to-do, others relatively poor. Overall, neither group has any important advantage in property valuation over the five decades. There is no steady expansion outward from the central city, with each new layer of growth manifesting a neat and tidy tax base increment. The historical approach prevents the imposition of a preconceived (and unreal) mold on the metropolitan area. A representation of the area, as it unfolds over time, may look a bit messy because of its refusal to accept neat classifications and familiar tags and convincing hypotheses, but it does have the saving feature of being accurate.

In addition to answering questions about increasing uniformity, the historical data on property values also confirm a point—a very important point—that has been suggested by others. It concerns the municipalities with the richest property tax base. With remarkable consistency, not only are the same communities at the head of the list year after year and decade after decade, but also the same kinds of community are there. These are the strongly industrialized suburbs and the very high income residential suburbs. In other words, the winners are those that specialize in one of these kinds of land use.

This matter of specialization according to property use is at the heart of the metropolitan problem. "Among the suburban communities [of Milwaukee County], there is a high degree of internal homogeneity as to land use types. Some suburbs tend to function as industrial areas, many as purely residential areas. There are few, if any, suburbs that have the diversity of land uses to be found in the City of Milwaukee and that are traditionally associated with an urban center."[8]

This tendency toward greater "internal homogeneity as to land use" has been commented on frequently of late in studies of metropolitan areas. With regard to New York, Vernon commented: "Within these metropolitan areas . . . one begins to see a greater and greater degree of differentiation and specialization."[9] In his San Francisco study Margolis found 'that dormitory cities are better off than balanced ones in terms of property tax base, and concludes: "The findings of this study cast doubt on the rationality of a program of encouraging industrial and commercial land use for suburbs."[10]

To move the examination of land use specialization out of the area of general impressions into that of quantifiable data, the localities of Milwaukee County have been divided into three economic groups similiar to the classifications used by Margolis. The following definitions have been used: (1) a community with more than 80 percent of its taxable property listed as residential is called residential; (2) a community with over 35 percent of its taxable property listed as manufacturing is called industrial; and (3) all others are listed as balanced. Because there were still a number of towns in Milwaukee County until the mid-1950s with more than one-fourth of their property in the agricultural classification and because of the distortions arising from the very large number of boundary changes in the county during the 1950s, the classification into economic groups is done for only the last six time periods (1960–70).

When the median property values of each group are com-

8. Metropolitan Study Commission, *An Analysis of Land Use and Zoning in Milwaukee County, Wisconsin* (Milwaukee: MSC, 1959), p. 16.

9. Raymond Vernon, *The Changing Economic Function of the Central City* (New York: Committee for Economic Development, 1959), pp. 13, 14. See also Charles M. Tiebout, "A Pure Theory of Local Expenditures," *The Journal of Political Economy* 64 (October 1956):416–24.

10. Julius Margolis, "Municipal Fiscal Structures in a Metropolitan Region," ibid., 65 (June 1957):236.

pared, the industrial suburbs and the residential suburbs take turns seizing the lead spot. If the mean of each group were used, the industrial suburbs would always be at the top. But what is particularly germane to the present discussion is the position of the balanced communities: they are always much poorer in property tax base than the two specialized types. In fact, the median property value of the balanced group consistently runs more than 50 percent below the average of the other two groups. And, what of the central city? It, of course, belongs in the balanced group of municipalities. Not only is it in this bottom group, but in every single time period, Milwaukee's tax base is below the median of the bottom group.

This economic specialization within a metropolitan area leads quite naturally into a high degree of competition among the localities. Wood remarks: "George A. Duggar has outlined the rationale which under the present system any prudent and responsible local official is led to adopt. Since the property tax is still the major single source of revenue, the obvious course of action for any single jurisdiction is to strive to attract the greatest possible amount of high-value property within its boundaries."[11] And Wood points to the obvious tools to be employed in this competition: "But by far the most effective weapons are the zoning and planning powers. Here the techniques which theoretically promise the most for orderly regional development are turned to provincial purposes and set to work to capture high-value property for individual municipalities."[12] The serious effects such competition will have on the basic economic unity of the area are clear. "There is among many of the municipalities of the county [Milwaukee] a competition for industry which has intensified the disunity and fragmentation of the natural metropolitan unit and has resulted generally in an illogical distribution of indus-

11. Wood, *1400 Governments*, p. 32. The reference is to George A. Duggar, "The Tax System and Responsible Housing Programs" (Ph.D. Diss., Harvard University, 1956).
12. Wood, *1400 Governments*, p. 33.

trial districts and occasionally in glaring examples of bad spot zoning."[13]

This reference to competition for industrial property should not be permitted to distract attention from the fact that the most serious policy issues involve competition for residential property.[14] Residential competition touches very directly on matters of human dignity and human rights. It is common knowledge that zoning laws are often used to exclude the poor, the elderly, the colored, the less educated. And yet, this is exactly what public "prudence" tells each local government to do.[15] Given the present splintering of metropolitan areas, it is obviously far more reasonable for those localities who can manage it to zone out residents who do not pay their way.

In existing circumstances, town fathers can scarcely afford not to practice discrimination. So long as all the industrial and residential land uses of the metropolitan region which, taken together, provide balance to the tax structure are not within one jurisdiction, a municipality which welcomes lower-income newcomers invites financial catastrophe. Common sense dictates that competition go on even if the result is to distort the process of industrial location, buttress impulses toward exclusiveness, and establish tax inducements and special privileges as permanent public policies.[16]

Further, the Wisconsin shared income tax (to be discussed in Chapter 5) provides still more motivation for specializing

13. Metropolitan Study Commission, *Land Use and Zoning in Milwaukee County*, p. iv.

14. In regard to this matter of competition for residential property, the Metropolitan Study Commission noted: "The basic problem results from ignoring the economic logicality of concentrated urban development and of unified metropolitan development in the rebellious flight of the middle and upper income classes to outer suburbia. The county, therefore, finds itself impaled on the horns of a perplexing dilemma—caught between the legitimate need to provide for medium and lower income housing, and the practical danger of economic chaos engulfing many municipalities if such development upsets the stability of the local tax base." Ibid., p. 39.

15. Ibid., p. 29.

16. Wood, *1400 Governments*, p. 34.

either in heavy industrial concentration (to obtain more corporate income taxes) or in exclusive high income residential suburbs (to obtain more individual income taxes).

The extensive data collected on property values also permit a check to be made between property tax base and certain urban characteristics. First, it was thought that population density might be inversely related to per capita property values.[17] Even though density probably would be more closely associated with expenditure patterns than with resources, still it was thought that the large building lots of wealthy residential suburbs[18] along with the large areas devoted to industrial zoning in the manufacturing suburbs might result in an inverse relation between population density and per capita property values. But this expectation was unfulfilled in Milwaukee County. Over the years there is no trace of any persistent relationship at all between these two factors. It will be recalled that population density correlated closely with the date of a locality's incorporation. Hence, the present finding of no correlation between population density and per capita property values reveals that there is also no correlation between a community's age and its per capita property values.

Next, it was thought that per capita property resources might be related to the absolute size of a locality, using the term "size" to mean both population and area size. This belief was based more on general impression and observation than on strict economic logic; in metropolitan situations there appeared to be a tendency for the smaller localities (smaller in both senses) to be richer in resources. Therefore, numerous simple rank correlations were run to test the relation of property values with area and with population.

Generally, there is not a significant correlation between

17. Without giving explicit references, Wood supports this expectation by remarking that "jurisdictions with the highest population densities . . . tend to rank at the bottom of all metropolitan municipalities so far as income or property valuation is concerned." Ibid., p. 23.

18. Margolis, "Municipal Fiscal Structures," p. 231, finds such a negative correlation between density and property tax base in the case of dormitory cities.

area and resources, although some negative correlation does exist. There is, however, a significant negative correlation between size of population and per capita property in this particular metropolitan area. A simple hint of this is the fact that in 1920 the six highest localities in property valuation all had less than 6,500 population, while the five lowest had over 6,500; in 1930 the five highest had less than 7,500 in population, while the five lowest all had over 7,500, and so on over the years. There seems to be no one explanation of this association between high property valuation and small population that holds up over time. It seems to be explained partly by the restrictive zoning of some suburbs, partly by the small land area of some suburbs, partly by the fact that only when there is a large population is there a high proportion of apartment houses, duplexes, boarding houses, and slums.

5 Nonproperty Resources

SINCE THERE are no local sales taxes or local income taxes in Wisconsin, the revenue sources treated in this chapter are primarily state shared taxes and state aids.

One might think that the income level of a community should be listed as a resource. This view is based on the oft-repeated statement that all taxes are ultimately paid out of income. Although there is much truth in the statement at the macro or national level, the relation between public resources and income becomes somewhat strained at the state level, and thinner still at the local level of government. Thus, the use of income as a measure of resources is often worse than uninformative; it can all too easily be the source of serious error.

What is being studied here is governmental ability to obtain funds—what I have elsewhere dealt with under the heading of "fiscal capacity."[1] Obviously, the local government collects its property tax on a factory whether the factory has any income this year or not. Milwaukee collects its property tax on an insurance company's skyscraper whether the income earned by the company goes to stockholders in Arizona or Florida. The local government collects its property tax on a house whether the furnished apartment upstairs is rented this year or not, whether the family head is employed or

1. Advisory Commission on Intergovernmental Relations, *Measuring the Fiscal Capacity and Effort of State and Local Areas* (Washington: ACIR, 1971). The principal authors were Allen D. Manvel and Donald J. Curran.

not, whether there are three income-earners in the family or only an elderly retired couple. And so on. Similarly, some state payments to local governments not only fail to follow the income level of a municipality, but rather the state payments often deliberately go in the opposite direction of the income level—one thinks of welfare payments and of equalizing state school aids.

In brief, it is not the personal economic well-being of the people that these two chapters on resources seek to examine, but rather the governmental or fiscal capacity of the municipal corporations. West Milwaukee, for example, has a personal income level well below the suburban average. Yet, its per capita capacity to support public services is fantastically superior to that of any other county jurisdiction; this is because of its very high industrial property tax base per person and because of the large amounts of coprorate income taxes returned by the state to the village treasury. West Milwaukee is but an extreme example. Many other instances could be offered to document the importance of distinguishing between income level and fiscal capacity. This chapter (like the previous one) is an investigation of fiscal capacity.

In the sense of resources, therefore, state-local financial relations become essential to the central question being studied. That is, do funds from the state aggravate or lessen fiscal homogeneity in the metropolitan area over time? The size of state payments has grown so notably that they cannot be passed over. Fabricant estimates that, for the whole nation, grants-in-aid amounted to about 7 percent of revenues in 1903 and 26 percent in 1942.[2] That proportion seems to have leveled off; it was 28 percent in 1965. There is added interest in this aspect of local finance arising from the recent spate of literature discussing the influence of state aids on local spending levels.[3]

2. Solomon Fabricant, *The Trend of Government Activity in the United States Since 1900* (New York: National Bureau of Economic Research, 1952), p. 40.

3. In the *National Tax Journal* alone, one can find this impressive list of articles in the last few years: Glenn W. Fisher, "Determinants of State and Local Government Expenditures: A Preliminary Analysis,"

Wisconsin has a well-earned reputation for progressive state government in general and for good financial relations with its local units in particular.[4] There is an amusing side to the report in which the Taxation Committee of the State Legislature pats itself on the back for "approving and endorsing a policy of financial home rule" in Wisconsin.[5] Apparently, the Committee saw no problem reconciling that ideal with its action two years earlier in which it flatly prohibited localities from taxing income.[6] Yet, it does remain true "that Wisconsin requires more of its local governments than other states generally, but also gives them more financial assistance to carry out their larger assignments."[7]

Shared Taxes

The shared-taxes method of having state funds flow to local units of government is not very common, and therefore it calls for a word or two of explanation. It is significantly different from the more usual state grant-in-aid mechanism, and it has its own set of advantages and disadvantages.[8] The characteristics that make shared taxes distinctive are these: (1)

---

14 (December 1961):349–55; Ernest Kurnow, "Determinants of State and Local Expenditures Reexamined," 16 (September 1963):252–55; Glenn W. Fisher, "Interstate Variation in State and Local Government Expenditure," 17 (March 1964):55–74; Seymour Sacks and Robert Harriss, "The Determinants of State and Local Government Expenditures and Intergovernmental Flows of Funds," ibid., pp. 75–85; Elliott R. Morss, "Some Thoughts on the Determinants of State and Local Expenditures," 19 (March 1966):95–103; Ira Sharkansky, "Some More Thoughts About the Determinants of Government Expenditures," 20 (June 1967):171–79.

4. William D. Knight, Staff Director, *Wisconsin Legislative Council, 1950 Report: Taxation* (Madison: State Legislature, 1950), p. 105.

5. Ibid., p. xl. (This statement is from the Taxation Committee's Report, not from the report of the research staff under Professor Knight.)

6. Cf. statutory citation in Chap. 4, n. 1.

7. Knight, *Wisconsin Legislative Council, 1950 Report*, p. xxxvii.

8. Lawrence Lee Pelletier, *Financing Local Government* (Brunswick, Maine: Bureau of Research in Municipal Government Publications, 1948), p. 17.

revenue is returned to the place of origin; (2) it is apportioned according to a fixed percentage of the tax in question; and (3) the purposes of the revenue are not specified by the collecting agency. Amid the welter of theoretical arguments for and against this procedure, it is well to keep in mind Harold Groves's comment: "The fiscal independence of the local units under sharing is about the same as that of a minor son placed upon a revocable allowance by a generous father."[9]

Just what taxes in Wisconsin come under the heading of shared taxes? In order of importance they are: the income tax, utilities taxes, the liquor tax, and fire insurance premium. Of these shared taxes, the income tax is far and away the most important; I shall deal only with that and with the tax on public utilities. The fire insurance item is less significant, while the liquor tax is distributed on a population basis and therefore is neutralized in our per capita figures.

Shared Income Tax

Both the individual income tax and the corporate income tax are shared with the municipality of origin. In the case of the individual income tax, "origin" means place where the income-earner resides, not where he earns the income. In the case of the corporate income tax, "origin" means the municipality in which the firm or economic activity is located, not where the income-earner (stockholder) resides. Since its inception in 1911, the income tax offers a good insight into the shifts in attitude that have colored Wisconsin intergovernmental fiscal relations. The original 1911 legislature made sharing the dominant factor, i.e., a device whereby revenue is collected for the local units through the more efficient machinery of the state.[10] Thus, 70 percent of the tax revenue was to be returned to the city, village, or town of origin, 20 percent to the county of origin, and only 10 percent re-

9. Harold M. Groves, *Financing Government* (6th ed; New York: Holt, Rinehart and Winston, Inc., 1964), p. 456.

10. Special Joint Committee of Wisconsin Legislature, Income Tax Bill (1087m-30), April 28, 1911.

tained by the state. This distribution formula was based on the 1910 percentages of all taxes collected in the state which were applied to local, county, and state purposes.[11]

The concept of a centrally collected and locally shared tax has been modified over time. Thus, a surtax was skimmed off the top by the state to pay a soldiers' bonus for a few years after World War I; then there was an emergency relief surtax in the depression; then a teachers' retirement surtax from 1943 until the tax revision in 1961. The old 1911 notion that the state should simply be the collection agent for local treasuries has been diluted most of all, however, by changes in the distribution formula itself. In 1925, the state's share of the pool went up from 10 percent to 40 percent (with the frequent surtaxes increasing that percentage). Then almost every session of the legislature during the 1960s reduced the local share still further, so that by 1970 municipalities of origin received back 23 per cent of the individual income tax and 39 percent of the corporate income tax.[12] Table 5 gives the per capita figures of the income tax returned to each locality from 1960 to 1970.[13]

The amounts of income tax returned to each of the county localities have expanded greatly over time. The suburbs as a group have seen this source of public funds increase fifteen-fold since the early 1920s. This growth is far greater than the modest fourfold increase in the per capita property values of the suburbs (Chapter 4). The enormous growth in personal income that this nation experienced over the past 50 years is news to nobody. Yet this fifteenfold increase happened during a time when the municipal share of the individual income tax was cut from 70 percent to 23 percent, which makes the increase more impressive.

The more industralized localities (like the city of Mil-

11. Ibid., p. 25.

12. The interested reader can trace the history in Section 71.14 of Wisconsin Statutes.

13. Figures for earlier years are recorded in Donald J. Curran, "The Financial Evolution of the Milwaukee Metropolitan Area" (Ph.D. Diss., University of Wisconsin, 1963).

waukee, Cudahy, West Allis, West Milwaukee) showed a predictably strong reaction to World War II and the Korean War. Even though property values and returned income tax both show the same patterns of response to general business conditions, a comparison of the two local resources reveals how much more sensitive income tax is to the phases of the business cycle. Further, even in the case of income taxes, the corporate tax is considerably more volatile than the individual income tax; a glance at the changes between 1966 and 1968 provides an illustration.

And what of our main question: is there a growing or lessening of uniformity in this aspect of local finance? To make allowance for the great dollar growth of this kind of local revenue, the coefficient of variation is used as a measure. The results appear in Table 6.

There are, perhaps, signs of a modest coming together of the municipalities in this kind of fiscal capacity. The average variation in the first 20 years was about 70, in the next ten years 60, and in the last ten years about 50. Almost surely this was the result of the disappearance of towns in the county. To the extent that this is the reason, further closing of the gap is not to be expected. The drop in variation between 1968 and 1970 is not a new trend, but simply the effect of the 1970 recession on corporate shared taxes, especially in the case of Glendale, which happens to be the Q_3 municipality. Although there appears to have been only a slight shift toward more similarity over the five decades, there are, nonetheless, some interesting fluctuations along the way.

Some of these shifts deserve comment. This is especially so of the two peaks of variation in 1935 and 1945. The great spread of 1935 is the result of the bottom quartile dropping away to literally almost nothing in returned income tax; the four lowest towns in 1935 received back 0, 10¢, 15¢ and 25¢ per capita that year! These four were still largely rural.[14]

14. It is not inconceivable that the farmers were upholding their tradition of under-reporting income. Cf. John F. Due, *Government Finance* (3rd ed.; Homewood, Ill.: Richard D. Irwin, Inc., 1963), p. 163.

TABLE 5
Per Capita Shared Income Tax (Individual and Corporate)
For Municipalities of Milwaukee County, 1960–1970

	1960			1962		
	Indiv.	Corp.	Total	Indiv.	Corp.	Total
Milwaukee	$12.46	$9.78	$22.24	$14.08	$8.73	$22.81
Bayside	69.59	—	69.59	84.62	1.65	86.27
Brown Deer	16.21	3.23	19.44	12.25	3.05	15.30
Cudahy	11.92	22.51	34.43	11.79	14.06	25.85
Fox Point	92.50	.92	93.42	114.49	1.82	116.31
Franklin	11.77	1.71	13.48	9.35	1.14	10.49
Glendale	18.52	39.18	57.70	27.69	38.20	65.89
Greendale	9.27	2.13	11.40	13.89	1.38	15.27
Greenfield	10.05	.72	10.77	10.91	.94	11.85
Hales Corners	19.32	1.71	21.03	23.29	2.13	25.42
Oak Creek	8.03	13.55	21.58	8.95	29.14	38.09
River Hills	211.49	1.51	213.00	262.08	1.72	263.80
St. Francis	8.61	5.48	14.09	8.40	5.11	13.51
Shorewood	46.58	1.56	48.14	47.19	2.49	49.68
S. Milwaukee	13.37	7.19	20.56	12.71	2.53	15.24
Wauwatosa	30.67	6.48	37.15	29.70	6.86	36.56
W. Allis	11.66	8.28	19.94	9.41	5.72	15.13
W. Milwaukee	11.47	118.88	130.35	10.80	78.45	89.25
Whitefish Bay	63.33	1.01	64.34	60.83	1.40	62.23
Suburbs Only	24.83	9.75	34.58	24.48	7.95	32.43
Entire County	15.78	9.78	25.56	17.11	8.50	25.61

	1964			1966		
	Indiv.	Corp.	Total	Indiv.	Corp.	Total
Milwaukee	$16.87	$11.55	$28.42	$20.57	$13.97	$34.54
Bayside	64.35	1.94	66.29	95.43	1.11	96.54
Brown Deer	13.29	6.57	19.86	15.89	6.13	22.02
Cudahy	16.70	12.74	29.44	21.05	14.08	35.13
Fox Point	87.98	1.63	89.61	114.91	2.22	117.13
Franklin	13.22	1.68	14.90	17.22	2.31	19.53
Glendale	31.03	40.14	71.17	33.03	49.08	82.11
Greendale	17.95	1.33	19.28	20.04	1.52	21.56
Greenfield	14.15	.75	14.90	17.33	1.51	18.84
Hales Corners	29.22	2.55	31.77	29.83	3.36	33.19
Oak Creek	11.98	54.35	66.33	16.56	60.70	77.26
River Hills	182.87	1.31	184.18	186.69	1.68	188.37
St. Francis	13.11	6.76	19.87	16.61	9.58	26.19
Shorewood	45.38	3.06	48.44	61.15	3.59	64.74
S. Milwaukee	16.71	9.14	25.85	20.35	19.60	39.95
Wauwatosa	32.24	8.78	41.02	36.72	12.64	49.36
W. Allis	16.66	7.66	24.32	20.40	12.43	32.83
W. Milwaukee	14.41	78.84	93.25	18.97	123.91	142.88
Whitefish Bay	53.92	1.63	55.55	67.18	2.22	69.40
Suburbs Only	26.32	10.35	36.67	30.73	14.42	45.15
Entire County	19.70	11.20	30.90	23.68	14.11	37.79

(Table continued on next page)

TABLE 5 (continued)

| | 1968 | | | 1970 | | |
	Indiv.	Corp.	Total	Indiv.	Corp.	Total
Milwaukee	$23.25	$13.50	$36.75	$26.15	$13.58	$39.73
Bayside	109.21	1.70	110.91	110.03	2.34	112.37
Brown Deer	22.95	4.18	27.13	32.65	8.15	40.80
Cudahy	24.44	20.48	44.92	26.96	11.34	38.30
Fox Point	151.22	2.11	153.33	131.83	1.62	133.45
Franklin	20.68	2.65	23.33	26.30	1.89	28.19
Glendale	46.26	45.19	91.45	50.89	29.21	80.10
Greendale	24.67	2.05	26.72	30.28	2.56	32.84
Greenfield	24.97	1.53	26.50	30.13	1.61	31.74
Hales Corners	37.52	3.83	41.35	41.54	3.75	45.29
Oak Creek	20.17	37.91	58.08	23.99	36.07	60.06
River Hills	247.27	1.52	248.79	231.31	1.72	233.03
St. Francis	19.33	7.37	26.70	23.89	6.62	30.51
Shorewood	62.90	3.79	66.69	74.50	3.63	78.13
S. Milwaukee	23.35	14.51	37.86	27.79	13.11	40.90
Wauwatosa	44.86	10.82	55.68	43.90	19.84	63.74
W. Allis	24.31	13.06	37.37	27.55	13.94	41.49
W. Milwaukee	24.90	102.00	126.90	27.19	77.03	104.22
Whitefish Bay	72.92	2.27	75.19	73.98	2.78	76.76
Suburbs Only	38.18	12.86	51.04	40.85	13.02	53.87
Entire County	27.92	13.30	41.22	30.85	13.40	44.25

Source: Income Tax Division, Wisconsin Department of Revenue (previously, Department of Taxation).

The rest of the county suffered a decrease in returned income tax in 1935 also, of course, but nothing like the tenfold drop of the bottom towns. The very high variations in 1945 on the other hand can be explained better in terms of the top quartile than the bottom. That is, the "richer" localities (in terms of shared income tax) increased more than four times their 1940 figure, while the bottom group was only doubling. The dramatic leap upward of the top quartile is largely attributable to the wartime income surge in the industrial suburbs of West Allis and West Milwaukee; they nudged two residential suburbs (Shorewood and Whitefish Bay) out of the top group under the impetus of war production. The decline from the high variation of 1945 is to be expected. The municipalities in the upper group could not continue the same rate of rapid growth they had known in wartime, so the rate of increase in the lower groups was proportionately

TABLE 6
Coefficients of Quartile Variation in
Per Capita Amounts of Returned Income
Tax for Municipalities of Milwaukee
County, 1925–1970

1925–1945		1945–1970	
Year	Coefficient	Year	Coefficient
1925	56.7	1950	72.2
1930	56.0	1952	65.6
1935	89.0	1954	60.1
1940	68.5	1956	60.0
1945	83.0	1958	54.2
		1960	61.6
		1962	62.3
		1964	53.9
		1966	51.6
		1968	54.2
		1970	35.3

Sources: data in Table 5; Donald J. Curran, "The Financial Evolution of the Milwaukee Metropolitan Area" (Ph.D. Diss., University of Wisconsin, 1963), pp. 111–14.

greater after 1945, resulting in a retreat from the artifically high variation of that year.

What of the relation between the central city and its satellities? The basic point is that the suburbs have had a definite advantage in this important source of revenue since 1935. The question of growing or lessening uniformity is not crystal clear in the past few time periods recorded in Table 5. Between 1960 and 1970, the central city has closed the gap somewhat. Yet, if one looks only at the very recent years, the suburbs have been increasing their advantage since 1964. The long-range view was the purpose of the study, however, and here there is clear evidence of a move toward less homogeneity. From the 1920s to 1970, the suburban average per capita shared income tax has grown 1,413 percent, whereas

Milwaukee's increased 937 percent. This growing advantage of the suburbs becomes more meaningful when we relate it to the similar movement of property resources described in the last chapter. In other words, state sharing of income taxes compounds the discrepancy which already exists between suburbs and central city in the matter of property tax base, and, in both cases, the disparity is worsening. Inasmuch as these are the main two resources of the county's municipalities, this kind of trend is disturbing.

Let the focus move to the question of greater or less fiscal homogeneity between groups divided according to their date of incorporation. Common sense would seem to suggest the same sort of pattern that had been expected (and not found) in the case of property values; namely that the older municipalities would have an early advantage in this kind of revenue source, but that the newer ones would gradually nibbble away that advantage. In the present case, that expectation is fulfilled. The two groups have drawn somewhat together over the past 50 years. The median of the municipalities which incorporated earlier has grown fourteenfold, while that of the younger municipalities—starting out intitially lower—has gained a bit by growing eighteenfold in the same period. Put another way, the younger localities had 69 percent as much shared income tax as the older ones in 1925 and they have 86 percent as much in 1970. This gradual catching up is normal as rural and unsettled areas evolve into residential communities appealing to upper income groups. Far more impressive than this rather slow move toward uniformity is the sharp closing of the gap between the two groups since 1945; in that year the younger localities received only 40 percent as much as the older (as compared with the 86 percent figure for 1970). Almost surely, the new communities appearing periodically on the metropolitan fringes will follow along in this trend toward greater similarity among the suburbs.

Shared income taxes manifest interesting patterns when local units of government are grouped in economic classes. The industrial group used to receive the largest amount per capita, but in recent years the median of the residential suburbs has taken the lead. Understandably, the payments made to industrial communities react far more than the others to depression, to war, to recession, to economic recovery, etc.; the corporate share is especially sensitive. The high degree of sensitivity to general business conditions points up the obvious difficulty of budgeting and long-range planning for these industrial suburbs. The balanced communities trail far behind the other two groups in per capita shared income taxes. Thus, just as the previous chapter suggested strong property tax reasons for municipalities to specialize, so now the shared income tax offers a further reason to specialize.

The central city is, of course, balanced in nature and suffers pretty much the same fate as the balanced group. The question arises whether the central cities around the country would not usually be of the balanced type. It seems likely. Since they are generally much older than the suburbs, they had already developed and acquired their personality long before there evolved the kind of specialized or mercantilist zoning we know today. As a result, they are probably balanced rather than specialized. Thus, the finding that Milwaukee shares the relative poverty of the balanced type of locality in both property base and in income may offer a hint about the source of the "fiscal crisis" of central cities.

Shared Utility Taxes

Although this source of local revenue is not insignificant, and although it clearly touches our basic question, it nonetheless requires but a brief treatment. Utility property (light, power, and heat) is assessed and taxed by the state government rather than by the municipality in which the plant happens to be located. Then the state distributes the taxes as follows: 65 percent to the municipality of origin, 20 percent to the county of origin, with 15 percent retained by the state. The municipality of origin means the place where the utility sells its gas or electricity and the place where the plant is located. The State Supreme Court has decreed that in distributing the local government's 65 percent share, a dollar of sales and a dollar of assessed property value shall be counted alike. Clearly, this means an enormous amount of funds from the state will go to the jurisdiction which contains the utility plant, whereas relatively small amounts will go to the rest of the jurisdictions wherein light, heat, and power are sold. The pertinent data on this matter appear in Table 7.

TABLE 7
Local Shares of State Utility Tax,
Selected Per Capita Figures in Milwaukee County,
1925–1970

Year	County Aver.	Suburb Aver.	Central City	Lake	Oak Creek	St. Francis
1925	1.35	1.76	1.25	11.74	1.15	—
1930	2.53	3.18	2.36	24.93	4.45	—
1935	2.14	3.63	1.73	30.97	5.63	—
1940	2.23	3.95	1.67	36.99	3.53	—
1945	2.21	3.01	1.94	21.18	2.53	—
1950	2.19	2.62	2.03	13.96	1.25	—
1952	2.31	2.60	2.20	17.09	1.67	—
1954	1.86	2.83	1.51	—	15.33	22.58
1956	2.80	5.49	1.86	—	109.83	21.51
1958	3.38	6.46	2.24	—	115.51	18.99
1960	4.30	8.35	2.69	—	142.87	15.90
1962	5.94	10.04	4.26	—	168.51	15.88
1964	6.72	10.95	4.92	—	164.91	15.25
1966	7.40	12.23	5.28	—	180.73	14.45
1968	9.14	14.55	6.68	—	209.77	16.54
1970	11.16	16.63	8.59	—	213.20	28.79

Source: Annual Report of the Clerk (Comptroller), Wisconsin Department of State Audit for selected years

The reason for choosing to study suburbs of Lake, Oak Creek, and St. Francis is clear from Chapter 3. Throughout most of the period of investigation, the only really large utility plant in the county was located in the town of Lake. Then, in 1951 the city of St. Francis deliberately incorporated itself around this utility plant, thereby depriving Lake of its main revenue source and inducing it to consolidate with the city of Milwaukee. A second (and much larger) power plant was begun in the town of Oak Creek in the early 1950s. Two results of this were: a decline in the value and use of the original power plant in St. Francis, and the incorporation of Oak Creek as a city. Apart from these "special" suburbs, the rest of the localities in the county generally receive roughly equal shares of this tax; the central city's share is a pretty good indicator of what that normal share was up until about 1952. There appears to be a slight trend away from uniformity in the amounts of this returned tax over the past 45 years. This trend exists whether the "bonanza" suburbs are included or not.

To better understand the fiscal evolution of the Milwaukee metropolitan area, it would be helpful to know whether the addition of the utility tax aggravates or lessens existing differences in resources among the municipalities. This, too, is a test of fiscal homogeneity, but used in a different manner than the one employed thus far. Normally, the question is raised whether there is a move toward or away from homogeneity over time; in this case we ask if the mere presence of the shared utility tax at any point in time results in more similarity of resources than its absence. Since most of the localities receive per capita amounts very similar to one another, the present question concerns primarily the three localities that have (or had) sizeable utility plants within their borders. In the case of these particular suburbs, does the large utility tax they receive bring them closer to the rest of the localities in overall fiscal resources or move them further away? All three "utility suburbs" were well below the suburban average in per capita property valuation during the period they were receiving the high utility taxes, except Oak Creek after 1962. Similarly, these three have been consistently below the suburban average in returned income taxes except for Oak Creek from 1960 onward. In general, then, the shared utility taxes had been reducing disparity in resources (accidentally, to be sure) through the 1930s, 1940s, and 1950s; but, since 1960, these state payments have been worsening disparity by enriching primarily a municipality that is already well off in property resources and in shared income taxes. This is the kind of finding that is useful for policy decisions in the Milwaukee County area, but that may have little applicability elsewhere.

If the suburbs with a utility windfall are removed from consideration, the rest of the suburbs have an average shared utility tax that is very close to that of Milwaukee. Thus, this shared tax does not make the central city and the suburbs as a group more or less like one another in resources, except that the windfalls do always end up somewhere in the suburbs.

State Grants-In-Aid

The second kind of "nonproperty resources" is the state system of grants. Perhaps the best way to understand the nature of this type of revenue is to contrast it with shared taxes, as described earlier: (1) aids are apportioned on the basis of need rather than as a fixed percentage of the tax yield; (2) aids are generally earmarked for specific purposes, whereas shared taxes are not; and (3) the aim of aids is to attain a certain equalization or to provide certain minimum standards of service, whereas a shared tax is simply supposed to return the revenue to its source.

For decades, scholars have discussed the advantages, justifications, dangers, etc., of state aids. All seem to agree that the main reason for employing state aids is to insure a basic level of services throughout the state in those areas which are thought to be of statewide interest.[15] To the extent that they are given on the basis of need, aids are a means of transferring funds from the wealthier portions of the state to the poorer. George Break, in a book written for the Brookings Institution

15. Compare, among others, J. A. Maxwell, "State Grants in Aid," *Bulletin of the National Tax Association* 33 (November 1947):33; L. L. Pelletier, *Financing Local Government*, p. 43; and note listing of justifications for grants on p. 48 ibid.

on intergovernmental fiscal relations, comes close to saying that external benefits or spillover effects are the only economic justification for categorical aids.[16] He is referring to the fact that the benefits of many services provided by local governments cannot be made to stay within the boundaries of the jurisdiction that supplies the service; daily commuting from one municpality to another is one reason for spillovers and the frequency with which the average American family changes its address (every five years) is another reason. On the critical side, there are very few who unequivocally and universally condemn aids. Rather, the criticism is of the way in which they are used or the degree to which they are used. Regarding the matter of degree, there is the danger of ossification of inefficient forms of government.[17] It is my impression that a growing number of experts in this field are swinging in the direction of favoring nonspecific grants. Carl Chatters was perhaps ahead of his time when he suggested in 1944 that, "It would help the cities and relieve the situation far more if grants-in-aid, when given, were made for very broad instead of limited purposes."[18]

The role played by state aids in Wisconsin is less important than in most other states. Major aids for localities consist of grants for education and for highways.[19] As is obvious, the aids are aimed at two of the services which are commonly thought to be of statewide interest. There will be no detailed

16. George F. Break, *Intergovernmental Fiscal Relations in the United States* (Washington, D.C.: The Brookings Institution, 1967). He makes this point repeatedly, especially in Chapter III (pp. 62–106).

17. "Finally the policy of distributing aid on the basis of need, unless there are some limitations, may perpetuate archaic, inefficient units of government." Institute of Training in Municipal Administration, *Municipal Finance Administration* (Chicago: International City Managers' Association, 1955), p. 51.

18. Carl H. Chatters, *Financing Local Improvements* (Chicago: American Public Works Administration, 1944), p. 8.

19. Omitted from consideration in this section are the grants which the state makes to the counties (especially for welfare), not because they are negligible, but because they do not affect our particular subject—the fiscal evolution of the municipalities in Milwaukee County.

quantitative treatment here of school aids. The reasons are numerous and cogent. The main reason is the simple fact that these aids are made not to the municipality but to the school district. In most cases, the boundaries of these districts have no relation to municipal boundaries. As late as 1950, when there were 18 localities in Milwaukee County, there were over 50 school districts. Therefore, to relate school aids to specific municipalities would involve such extensive extrapolation that resulting figures would be misleading rather than informative. This is especially true when there have been literally hundreds of municipal boundary changes in recent decades by annexation, consolidation, and incorporation.

Briefly, then, the educational aids are of two major kinds: flat aids and equalization aids. The former are fixed sums of money per pupil granted to all school districts which have more than the minimum amount of equalized property valuation per pupil. The equalization aids, on the other hand, go to those school districts which do not have this minimum; they are aimed at increasing the ability of the poorer districts to supply a satisfactory level of instruction. Thus, the latter are not fixed sums but vary with each district in accordance with its assessed property valuation and also in accordance with its local efforts to achieve quality. The two kinds of aid are mutually exclusive; no school district receives both of them.

Fortunately, this necessity of omitting educational grants from the investigation of revenue sources is not a serious deficiency in the case of Milwaukee County. Of the two types of educational aids (flat grants and equalization grants), Milwaukee County districts receive predominantly the former. Therefore, these aids would have little effect in changnig the resource position of any locality in the county. Much like the shared liquor tax, which is distributed on a per capita basis, the impact of school aids can be presumed to be relatively neutral for our purposes, especially in the later years.

The highway aids are something else again. Even though they are not a large item, they do go directly to each locality, and they do differ from one community to another because of local conditions (e.g, population, number of vehicles registered in a locality, number of miles of streets, etc.).

For present purposes, the analysis of state highway aids to localities begins with the year 1935. Leaving out of account a number of insignificant aids, there are two main types: the highway privilege tax allotment, and the local road and street allotment. The first of these was enacted in 1931 to replace the revenue lost by municipalities when automobiles were removed from the property tax roles in that year. The second aid is now of two types: the basic (fixed) allotment and the supplemental (varying) amount added in accordance with the amount left each year in the state highway fund for this purpose. The local road and street allotment allocates a certain number of state dollars for each mile of streets, depending on the kind of municipality that receives the aid. Towns and villages receive the least, and, among the four city classes, the larger the city population the more dollars are granted per dollar of streets.

In 1958 the Metropolitan Study Commission (created and supported during its brief life span by the state legislature) put out a report on motor vehicle costs and revenues as they related to Milwaukee County. This report noted that the residents of the county receive back only one dollar in state highway aids for every three they pay in motor vehicle taxes.[20] The situation in the central city was described thus: in 1958, the city of Milwaukee was expected to spend $43.81 more per registered vehicle than would be realized from vehicle-generated revenue.[21]

Table 8 gives the per capita amounts of highway aids received by each locality in the last 10 years.[22] State imposition of motor fuel taxes has pushed up the size of this grant-in-aid from what it was in the early years of the study. This source of revenue is quite a bit smaller than the shared income tax

20. Metropolitan Study Commission, "Report on Motor Vehicle Taxation," Mimeographed (Milwaukee, July 28, 1958), p. ii.

21. Ibid., p. 2.

22. Data for earlier years are available in Curran, "Financial Evolution of the Milwaukee Metropolitan Area."

TABLE 8
Per Capita Highway Aids for Municipalities of
Milwaukee County, 1960–1970

	1960	1962	1964	1966	1968	1970
Milwaukee	$5.71	$5.80	$6.67	$7.15	$7.64	$8.19
Bayside	8.12	8.34	8.40	8.79	9.60	9.95
Brown Deer	4.34	4.85	5.59	5.94	6.65	7.70
Cudahy	5.23	4.97	5.39	5.67	5.86	6.33
Fox Point	6.70	7.02	7.60	8.00	8.67	9.23
Franklin	9.50	10.91	11.34	11.67	12.17	12.61
Glendale	7.34	8.23	8.48	9.03	8.81	9.22
Greendale	6.58	7.03	6.74	7.15	7.39	7.84
Greenfield	8.00	7.52	7.61	7.59	7.61	8.08
Hales Corners	8.29	8.50	8.65	8.97	9.22	9.74
Oak Creek	8.86	9.11	9.54	10.22	9.51	11.82
River Hills	15.12	16.54	17.00	19.82	19.02	22.59
St. Francis	3.63	4.30	4.72	4.92	5.09	5.68
Shorewood	3.81	4.03	4.29	4.50	4.66	5.20
S. Milwaukee	5.66	5.44	5.69	5.83	6.09	6.36
Wauwatosa	7.48	7.20	7.75	8.24	8.59	9.09
W. Allis	6.66	6.45	6.99	7.36	7.63	8.29
W. Milwaukee	7.14	7.54	7.93	9.48	9.93	11.54
Whitefish Bay	3.53	3.72	4.08	4.32	4.69	5.17
Suburbs Only	6.48	6.54	6.36	7.36	7.69	8.25
Entire County	5.93	6.02	6.76	7.21	7.65	8.21

Source: Annual Report of Clerk (Comptroller) from each locality, Municipal Audit Division, Department of Administration, State of Wisconsin.

for all county municipalities, but larger than the shared utility tax in the majority of them. Simple observation, coupled with examination of coefficients of variation, suggest that there has been a definite and consistent trend toward greater uniformity in per capita highway aids among the localities over the past 35 years. It seems quite clear that this trend has been accelerated by the disappearance of towns.

In examining the relation of the central city to the suburbs as a group, two points should be kept in mind: (1) the central city receives considerably more in aids per mile of streets than does any suburb because of its large population size; and (2) Milwaukee has far fewer miles of streets per capita than its suburbs as a group (in 1950 Milwaukee had 0.0013 miles per person and the suburbs had 0.0035). The first of these points would give the central city a definite advantage over its suburbs, whereas the second works against the central city when aids are considered in per capita terms. In the early years of the study, the central city consistently received more aids per capita than the suburbs. More recently, the two contrary forces mentioned above cancelled one another out, so that the central city and the suburban average are quite close to one another. This should not mask a 4 to 1 spread among the suburbs.

The latest of the state aids is called "Property Tax Relief" or "Property Tax Credit." It was enacted in the early 1960s and, in the two-year intervals of this study, shows up first in 1964. A sum of money determined by the legislature is allocated each year to the property tax relief fund. The share going to individual localities depends on the number of mills of total tax rate that localities levy over and above a statutory base. By setting the base at 14 mills, the statute assured that all 19 municipalities of Milwaukee County receive a share of the fund, since the lowest total rate found among them since 1964 was 23 mills. The per capita dollar amounts going to each municipality appear in Table 9.

In each time period, the two localities receiving the largest per capita amounts of relief are either first and second or first and third in per capita property wealth. The three localities receiving the smallest per capita credit always include the two poorest in terms of per capita property values. The credit funds come from the state sales tax. Most public finance economists rank the property tax somewhat below the sales tax as a rational and equitable revenue instrument. In that respect, something good can be said for the property tax credit. To the extent, however, that property tax relief might be thought of as an appropriate measure to help those who are weak in property tax base, the two poorest jurisdictions (St. Francis and Franklin) should be receiving proportion-

TABLE 9
**Per Capita Amounts of Property Tax Credit Payments
to Municipalities of Milwaukee County, 1964–1970**

	1964	1966	1968	1970
Milwaukee	$30.32	$33.11	$40.22	$43.94
Bayside	24.27	24.67	31.55	34.93
Brown Deer	17.30	21.41	25.28	34.89
Cudahy	33.08	42.02	47.14	54.15
Fox Point	27.65	25.98	26.64	30.57
Franklin	16.64	15.70	15.42	18.79
Glendale	52.06	49.90	64.99	75.73
Greendale	20.74	15.45	19.74	24.60
Greenfield	15.53	17.07	22.92	28.29
Hales Corners	27.31	24.92	24.91	24.26
Oak Creek	26.58	26.76	30.42	43.65
River Hills	47.79	34.17	36.91	43.24
St. Francis	13.74	15.93	17.53	19.57
Shorewood	19.48	19.59	21.84	23.37
S. Milwaukee	30.78	29.23	29.68	31.00
Wauwatosa	23.67	27.82	34.98	39.83
W. Allis	41.81	39.34	49.89	52.38
W. Milwaukee	143.92	186.66	232.06	347.50
Whitefish Bay	19.27	19.71	22.05	24.70
Suburbs Only	30.17	31.25	37.47	43.17
Entire County	30.27	32.54	39.36	43.69

Source: Municipal Audit Division, Department of Administration, State of Wisconsin.

ately more per capita than the others instead of consistently receiving the least.

Apart from shared taxes and aids, the other major nonproperty type of local resources would include such methods of raising money as charges, fees, fines, special assessments, departmental earnings, gifts, etc. When summed together, they produce a total (for some localities in particular) that is not inconsiderable. Nonetheless, they are omitted inasmuch as these sources of revenue are not truly different kinds of "resources." The fact that a particular municipality chooses to pay for a new sewer extension by assessing the property owners affected rather than by the general property tax certainly does affect the tax rate, but it does not mean that the community is any richer or poorer in resources than if it paid for the sewer by general taxes.

Relation of Property and Nonproperty Resources

An understanding of the ability of the Milwaukee metropolitan communities to support local services requires some unified comprehension of state payments and property tax base. Similarly, any judgment about the effectiveness, equity, or rationality of the Wisconsin system of payments to localities can be made only when these payments are related to the property base they complement.

An obvious difficulty presents itself when we try to compare property values with state revenues, for the former are potential sources of revenue whereas the latter are actual receipts in local treasuries. To put the two on a comparable basis, I took the average total property tax rate of all the county municipalities in each time period and multiplied this by the per capita property valuations of each locality, as shown in Table 2. The results become column (1) in Table 10, thus, this column is just a reflection of Table 2. Of course, these figures are not the amounts which each municipality actually raised by the property tax. Yet, they are quite meaningful in that they represent what each locality would have (could have) raised if they all employed the same property tax rate. Since our discussion in the past two chapters has been of resources, of fiscal capacity, these figures have real significance. Column (2) of each time period is the simple sum (per capita) of the state payments we have here considered: shared income tax, shared utility tax, highway aids, and property tax credit. Column (3) is the sum of columns (1) and (2). Thus, all three columns are on a per capita basis.

Do the state payments increase or lessen uniformity among the localities? To answer this, the quartile coefficients of variation of column (3) for each time period were computed; they are reproduced in Table 11. The first column of this table is the coefficient of variation for property valuations; the second column lists the coefficients of variation after the state payments.

One point that emerges from Table 11 is the rather small change in variation that the addition of the state payments makes. The other point that emerges, and it is an important point, is the fact that the variation is consistently higher after the state payments over the past 20 years. This suggests that state payments come to the localities, particularly in more recent years, largely in proportion to the property values those localities possess. It means that the most is received by the wealthiest and the least by the poorest. It means further that the overall effect of these payments is to intensify whatever inequalities were already there in property values. This relationship is not so marked before 1945, but from 1950 on rank correlations show a very significant connection between property valuations and the sum of the state payments.

The recently enacted property tax credit has been added into the state payments, of course, only in the last four time periods. For comparison purposes, the coefficient of variation was measured both with the credit included and with it omitted. The addition of the credit has practically no effect at all on the amount of variation. Since it was not intended to be an equalizing instrument, it should not be condemned for failing to operate as such. It is interesting, however, to see that, even in its most recent aid program, the state government continues its earlier pattern of giving more dollars per capita to the fiscally rich municipalities and less to the fiscally poor ones.

The tendency of the state receipts to follow property base can be expressed in another way. I went through all the time periods since 1925 to find out how often the state receipts equalized the imbalance already existing in property values and how often they exaggerated the imbalance. Over the whole 45 years, 70 percent of the localities received state funds that heightened their property advantage or disadvantage. As a group, the high income residential suburbs come out best in per capita amounts of state payments.

TABLE 10
Per Capita Dollar Amounts of Potential Property Tax Yields at Average Countywide Rates and of Actual State Payments, Municipalities in Milwaukee County,
1960–1970

	1960			1962		
	Property Capacity	State Payments	Total Resources	Property Capacity	State Payments	Total Resources
	(1)	(2)	(3)	(1)	(2)	(3)
Milwaukee	$151.74	$31.55	$183.29	$171.64	$32.87	$204.51
Bayside	295.71	88.83	384.54	342.10	98.54	440.64
Brown Deer	161.01	23.06	184.07	141.20	23.43	164.63
Cudahy	200.96	29.66	230.62	234.16	34.83	268.99
Fox Point	298.22	115.72	413.94	337.45	127.60	465.05
Franklin	127.67	24.45	152.12	140.09	26.70	166.79
Glendale	413.55	65.12	478.67	480.45	82.33	562.78
Greendale	130.33	22.03	152.36	159.67	25.14	184.81
Greenfield	136.67	23.79	160.46	151.08	22.70	173.78
Hales Corners	193.60	34.26	227.86	215.63	37.09	252.72
Oak Creek	197.94	186.15	384.09	235.34	215.71	451.05
River Hills	446.17	287.25	733.42	510.27	286.67	796.94
St. Francis	103.78	33.68	137.46	126.12	33.69	159.81
Shorewood	175.87	59.56	235.43	196.80	57.17	253.97
S. Milwaukee	157.84	24.47	182.31	182.37	23.54	205.91
Wauwatosa	211.69	47.28	258.97	248.98	47.18	296.16
W. Allis	205.29	32.49	237.78	226.58	26.01	252.59
W. Milwaukee	832.51	141.22	973.73	982.49	111.64	1,094.13
Whitefish Bay	204.52	75.10	279.62	227.70	68.51	296.21
Suburbs Only	209.00	48.72	257.72	237.08	42.88	279.96
Entire County	168.04	35.44	203.48	190.73	35.79	226.52

	1964			1966		
	Property Capacity	State Payments	Total Resources	Property Capacity	State Payments	Total Resources
	(1)	(2)	(3)	(1)	(2)	(3)
Milwaukee	$189.32	$70.33	$259.65	$206.68	$80.08	$286.76
Bayside	368.09	103.19	471.28	402.07	134.36	536.43
Brown Deer	157.99	46.15	204.14	200.53	53.08	253.61
Cudahy	267.59	72.38	339.97	309.69	87.86	397.55
Fox Point	367.70	129.54	497.24	409.83	156.02	565.85
Franklin	151.26	49.23	200.49	169.92	53.83	223.75
Glendale	535.81	146.81	682.62	599.14	155.63	754.77
Greendale	170.73	49.66	220.39	192.85	47.29	240.14
Greenfield	163.26	41.67	204.93	183.09	47.26	230.35
Hales Corners	231.30	71.89	303.19	242.90	71.27	314.17
Oak Creek	286.28	267.36	553.64	316.46	294.97	611.43
River Hills	558.97	256.28	815.25	602.17	250.02	852.19
St. Francis	144.79	53.58	198.37	157.03	61.49	218.52
Shorewood	211.07	76.08	287.15	251.96	92.91	344.87
S. Milwaukee	202.24	65.70	267.94	215.45	78.79	294.24
Wauwatosa	283.80	76.49	360.29	328.51	90.04	418.55
W. Allis	261.78	78.27	340.05	285.96	85.28	371.24
W. Milwaukee	1,082.50	261.19	1,343.69	1,253.62	357.75	1,611.37
Whitefish Bay	251.48	81.86	333.34	279.99	96.79	376.78
Suburbs Only	266.46	84.15	350.61	298.37	95.99	394.36
Entire County	212.36	74.65	287.01	234.71	84.94	319.65

(Table continued on next page)

TABLE 10 (continued)

	1968			1970		
	Property Capacity	State Payments	Total Resources	Property Capacity	State Payments	Total Resources
	(1)	(2)	(3)	(1)	(2)	(3)
Milwaukee	$258.96	$91.29	$350.25	$302.13	$100.45	$402.58
Bayside	493.23	157.07	650.30	569.35	163.15	732.50
Brown Deer	294.24	63.71	357.95	386.91	89.35	476.26
Cudahy	373.01	103.96	476.97	420.44	106.08	526.52
Fox Point	494.65	194.20	688.85	574.82	179.85	754.67
Franklin	212.80	59.05	271.85	265.50	69.78	335.28
Glendale	744.09	181.00	925.09	845.49	181.61	1,027.10
Greendale	254.45	57.57	312.02	355.45	70.63	426.08
Greenfield	238.61	61.51	300.12	312.78	73.94	386.72
Hales Corners	309.83	80.38	390.21	379.06	85.30	464.36
Oak Creek	471.17	307.78	778.95	526.04	328.73	854.77
River Hills	703.65	313.51	1,017.16	826.01	309.34	1,135.35
St. Francis	199.28	65.86	265.14	233.56	84.55	318.11
Shorewood	320.51	97.95	418.46	384.32	112.18	496.50
S. Milwaukee	268.42	77.91	346.33	309.29	82.50	391.79
Wauwatosa	433.76	104.82	538.58	521.98	119.84	641.82
W. Allis	372.04	101.47	473.51	450.52	110.00	560.52
W. Milwaukee	1,577.84	390.32	1,968.16	1,868.69	490.11	2,358.80
Whitefish Bay	344.48	105.94	450.42	422.72	111.39	534.11
Suburbs Only	383.47	110.75	494.22	458.71	121.92	580.63
Entire County	297.86	97.37	395.23	352.17	107.31	459.48

Source: author's calculations from data presented in Tables 2, 5, 7, 8, and 9.

What was found here for Milwaukee County was also found by Knight for the whole state of Wisconsin. And what he says about comparisons of counties within the state is certainly applicable to comparisons of localities within Milwaukee County.

It is clear, however, that the normal income tax base is highly correlated with the property tax base, and that this association is strong enough so that high shared taxes per capita (except for counties in which liquor or utility taxes are significant) are generally found in counties in which full value per capita is also high. Thus, from the point of view of using income tax revenues for

TABLE 11
Coefficients of Quartile Variation in Per Capita
Property Valuations Alone and in Per Capita Property
Valuations Plus Per Capita State Payments for
Municipalities of Milwaukee County, 1925–1970

Year	Property Valuations Alone	Property Valuations Plus State Payments
	(1)	(2)
1925	31.6	31.9
1930	39.3	36.2
1935	42.8	40.2
1940	35.5	28.9
1945	43.3	38.1
1950	39.0	42.2
1952	30.8	34.3
1954	31.5	34.0
1956	35.1	38.9
1958	33.0	29.5
1960	32.1	35.7
1962	35.8	41.9
1964	36.6	38.3
1966	33.4	39.9
1968	31.1	33.2
1970	23.6	33.4

Sources: (1) Table 3; (2) Table 10, and Donald J. Curran,
"The Financial Evolution of the Milwaukee Metropolitan
Area" (Ph.D. Diss., University of Wisconsin, 1963). pp.
135–40.

property tax relief where relief is most needed, shared taxes are
much less effective than state aids.[23]

The relation of the central city to the suburb is interesting.
A comparison in Table 10 of the state payments received
by Milwaukee with those in the row marked "Entire County"

23. W. D. Knight, *Property Taxation and the Wisconsin Tax System*
(Madison: University of Wisconsin Bureau of Business Research and
Service, 1960), p. 122.

indicates that this revenue source has only had the effect of furthering the trend found in property values. That is, the central city's gradual worsening in property tax base related to its suburbs is matched by a gradual worsening in state payments also. Thus, the position of the central city in column (3) of Table 10 is generally a little more at a disadvantage related to the suburbs than it was in column (1). If one felt that something should be done to compensate the city of Milwaukee for the relative deterioration of its property base, then the present system of state payments is certainly not the way to go about it.

One last question growing out of this table deserves attention: Has the role played by these state receipts grown relative to property tax receipts over the period of investigation, and if so, by how much? That question cannot be answered individually for each locality from Table 10, because columns (1) and (3) are not actual revenues, but potential revenues interpolated from the average property tax rate for all the localities in the county. The figures in the bottom row marked "Entire County" however, are the actual figures for all three columns. Comparing the figures in this row over the 16 time periods gives a general answer to the question. Table 12 shows state payments as a percent of property taxes for each time period.

Table 12 indicates that there has been a notable increase proportionately in the part of local revenue supplied by payments from the state. The growth in their proportionate share takes on more significance when it is recalled that property values have increased more than 700 percent in the last 30 years; yet, even measured on this greatly expanded base, the state receipts managed to increase impressively. The jump between 1962 and 1964 is the result of the property tax credit.

In general, the last two chapters have demonstrated considerable variation in local resources among Milwaukee County municipalities, with no tendency for that variation to lessen over time. The fact that this inequality did not decrease during the steady urbanization process of the last five decades was hardly to be expected, especially when the addi-

TABLE 12
State Payments As Percent of
Average Property Tax

1925–1945		1950–1970	
Year	Percent	Year	Percent
1925	12	1950	23
1930	16	1952	28
1935	12	1954	32
1940	15	1956	26
1945	28	1958	24
		1960	21
		1962	19
		1964	35
		1966	36
		1968	33
		1970	30

Sources: Table 10, and Donald J. Curran,
"The Financial Evolution of the Milwaukee
Metropolitan Area" (Ph.D. Diss., University
of Wisconsin, 1963), pp. 135–40.

tion of new metropolitan fringes had been deliberately excluded. It seems that the most influential factor in this continuation of fiscal disparities was the development of economic specialization among the localities. The economic balance or mix of the central city and most of the older localities is not to be found in the newer ones. There are no current indications that this process of specialization with its concomitant inequality is slowing down.

6 Expenditures

THE WORD "financial" was discussed in Chapter 2 in the form of two questions: (1) where do the municipalities of Milwaukee County obtain their revenue; and (2) how do they spend it? Now that a general answer to the first question has been assembled, it is time to move on to the second.

Nearly all of the data underlying this chapter was obtained from the annual audit reports which each municipal government is required by law to submit to the state Municipal Audit Division shortly after the end of the fiscal year.[1] Use of this source has the advantage that the figures have already been checked for mechanical and human errors. Of far greater importance and value is the fact that a common classification and reporting system is thereby achieved. Since the purpose of this investigation is to make comparisons among municipalities, consistency is essential.

After much consultation, I decided to employ expenditure figures in each time period that were a sum of both operational costs and capital outlays. The investigation would have been too overloaded with numbers if separate treatment were accorded to operating costs, capital outlays, and total expenditures for each of five functions in each of 19 municipalities in each of 17 time periods; a choice had to be made between

1. In an administrative rearrangement, the pertinent section of the former Department of State Audit has become the Municipal Audit Division. The personnel in this section, particularly Mr. John Lunenschloss, have been especially helpful during the years that this study was in preparation.

using only operational expenditures or a total figure embracing operating and capital expenditures. One might argue that inclusion of capital outlays would make the figures lumpy and, therefore, misleading. That danger does not appear at all serious. Since 17 different time periods are employed for each locality and each expenditure class, the trend lines are clear and readily distinguishable. Further, the lumpiness is one of the very items being investigated; we want to know when money was paid out for major construction on streets, schools, sewers, etc. This information is necessary to understand the evolution of the county municipalities and is necessary to forecast the likely fiscal paths of newly emerging fringe localities outside the county. I kept a separate record of sizeable capital outlays each time that they occurred; in the rare cases when inclusion of capital outlays would be misleading, explicit reference will be made to the fact.[2]

The five local functions being studied in detail are general government, protection (police and fire), sanitation, highways, and education. These services provide a solid picture of a municipality's spending, since they are all both major and common functions. In the earlier stages of the study, an analysis was also made of debt service and of a spending category called "miscellaneous."[3] Although these items are not

2. In comparing one study with another, it is important to know whether capital outlays are being included or not. Thus, in the Cleveland study (on which Jesse Burkhead, "Uniformity in Governmental Expenditures and Resources in a Metropolitan Area: Cuyahoga County," *National Tax Journal* 14 [December 1961]: 337–48, is based) and in Harvey E. Brazer, *City Expenditures in the United States* (New York: National Bureau of Economic Research, 1959), capital outlays were not included; they were included, however, in Stanley Scott and Edward L. Feder, *Factors Associated with Variations in Municipal Expenditure Levels* (Berkeley: University of California Press, 1957).

3. The interested reader can follow the treatment of these two classes of local spending up to 1960 in Donald J. Curran, "The Financial Evolution of the Milwaukee Metropolitan Area" (Ph.D. Diss., University of Wisconsin, 1963).

When we come to speak of total expenditures later in this chapter, the data on debt service and miscellaneous are omitted for years up to 1960 in order that the total categories consistently embrace the same individual functions over the entire five decades.

insignificant, they required so much extrapolation and arbitrariness that it was decided to omit them.

General Government

This category refers to the costs involved in the administration of local governments. Most of the costs are for annual operation rather than capital outlays, for it is possible to build only so many city or village halls per community.

One point about general government spending should be stressed at the outset. Historically, per capita expenditures for this service fall into two neat halves: in the first half of the study period up to 1945, spending stayed remarkably constant, whereas in the second half of the study period it has soared upward. The reason for stressing the point is that this pattern repeats itself for every expenditure category to be examined in the pages that follow; by highlighting it early, I eliminate the need to repeat it each time. It is particularly important to recall this point when mention is made of spending growth rates. For example, to say that per capita general government expenditures have increased 540 percent in the county over the last five decades is really equivalent to saying that they have increased about 540 percent in the last 25 years (1945–70). Perhaps this recent burst in local spending, contrasted with earlier decades of stability, explains in part the citizen mood characterized in the 1960s as "taxpayer revolt."

To put expenditures for general government in perspective, it is helpful to see how large a role they play in local finance. In 1925, general government expenditures were 6 percent of total spending in the county on the five functions being considered; in 1970, the figure was 5 percent. Thus, its share of total spending (a modest one) has stayed quite constant over the 45 years.

Is there any increase in uniformity as far as spending on this service is concerned? To test this, the quartile coefficients of variation are offered in Table 13. The figures indicate that there has been no clear trend one way or the other. This came as a surprise, for it seemed reasonable to expect that

TABLE 13
Coefficients of Quartile Variation in
Per Capita General Government
Expenditures for Municipalities of
Milwaukee County, 1925–1970

1925–1945		1950–1970	
Year	Coefficient	Year	Coefficient
1925	31	1950	40
1930	28	1952	42
1935	28	1954	38
1940	33	1956	44
1945	17	1958	34
		1960	35
		1962	41
		1964	36
		1966	45
		1968	37
		1970	30

Source: Annual Report of Clerk (Comp-
troller) from each locality, Municipal Audit
Division, Department of Administration,
State of Wisconsin.

growing urbanization of the whole area—especially the disappearance of towns—would lead to greater homogeneity in
expenses for local administration. Such is apparently not the
case. Burkhead's search for growing uniformity in the Cleveland area was also inconclusive. He found a little increase
in homogeneity among the cities and a considerable decrease
in homogeneity among the villages over time.[4]

And now, on to the interesting matter of comparisons between the central city and suburbs in this function. The central
city's per capita expenditures for general government as a
percentage of the suburbs' per capita expenditures are shown
in Table 14. The central city generally spends less than the
suburbs taken as a group. This was perhaps to be expected,

4. Burkhead, "Uniformity in Governmental Expenditures and Resources," p. 344.

TABLE 14
City of Milwaukee's Per Capita
Expenditures for General Government as
a Percentage of Suburban Per Capita
Expenditures, 1925–1970

1925–1945		1950–1970	
Year	Percentage	Year	Percentage
1925	78	1950	111
1930	86	1952	96
1935	86	1954	76
1940	80	1956	79
1945	80	1958	140
		1960	100
		1962	86
		1964	91
		1966	98
		1968	99
		1970	77

Source: Annual Report of Clerk (Comp-
troller) from each locality, Municipal Audit
Division, Department of Administration,
State of Wisconsin.

inasmuch as this is the local service in which economies of
scale are most likely. The upswing in 1958 and 1960 appears
to be temporary; it can be traced to capital expenses. In any
case, the city of Milwaukee is never among the top five
spenders in this category, even in the years when it rose
above the suburban average (1950 and 1958).

Nevertheless, the central city appears in recent years to
enjoy less of an advantage in the costs of this service than
it did during the early decades of the study. To that extent,
there is not a truly solid basis here for the contention that
integration of the whole county will lead to a saving of tax
dollars by reason of the greater efficiency and economy that
size will bring. (This is independent, of course, of the related
contention that even if size doesn't bring economies, ending
the duplication of governmental services might well do so.)

Some hypotheses should be tested in the effort to better understand the factors influencing (or, at least, associated with) spending patterns. Simple rank correlations have been used to test for such factors. This kind of tool can do little more than give a hint that association does or does not exist. Yet, it serves a real purpose, for in a small universe like the 19 municipalities of Milwaukee County, it is possible to bring a great deal of detailed knowledge to bear in interpreting the correlations.

The first hypothesis is this: per capita expenditures for general government are positively associated with the age of a community, with age being determined by date of incorporation. In the earlier years the older group could be expected to spend more for this function, while in the later years this difference might well fade out and disappear. The reasons are twofold, although closely related: the minimum legal requirements set by the state for town administration are lower than for incorporated localities; and a rural area would call for proportionately less complicated machinery, since relatively few local services are administered. Yet, as the towns become more densely populated and gradually disappear, both of these reasons would lose force, leading one to expect a level of expenditures for government in the younger group rising closer to that of the older localities. It turns out that the towns are consistently the lowest per capita spenders right up to 1954; at least the bottom four out of five localities are towns in every time period.

When the medians of the two groups are traced over 45 years, the pattern is what would have been anticipated on a common sense basis. The older communities spent more per capita for local government up to 1952 (with the exception that the younger group went 3¢ ahead in 1945). But then, from 1954 onward, the younger municipalities are consistently above the older. Thus, it appears that a new municipality on the outskirts of a metropolitan area can expect its temporary saving in the matter of expenditures for local government to disappear over time.

The age of a locality and its type of political organization,

however, do not go far enough in explaining the notable variations in spending on this service. Is it possible to pin down
the reason for the wide differences at any one point of time?
The answer appears to be a rather simple and straightforward
one: resources. It is revenue sources that show the clos-
est and strongest relationship with per capita spending on
general government. The degree of rank correlation between
expenditures for general government and resources is very
high; it overrides age, type of political organization (incorporated or unincorporated), area size, economic type, population size, etc. Thus in those cases where some towns wander
off and depart from their usual pattern of low spending for
this function, the departure can nearly always be traced to
the resources of that town at that period. This relationship,
of course, has a policy implication. To the extent that the
spending of money is necesary for "good" local government,
it is unfortunate to find this function showing such close correlation with (dependence on?) the local resources of a
community.

It seemed logical to expect that as population density increased, per capita expenditures for local government would
go down. Presumably, much of the core of local government
would remain the same as population increased and, therefore, per capita costs would drop. This expectation was unfulfilled. Instead of a negative correlation between government expenditures and population density, there emerged in
nearly all time periods a positive correlation, although not
a significant one. Brazer also found this positive association.[5]

Protection

Protection includes expenditures for the police department,
fire department, licensing bureau, traffic control, etc. This
service takes a considerably larger slice from the local expenditure pie than general government, and its slice has been
getting bigger. In 1925, protection accounted for 13 percent

5. Brazer, *City Expenditures in the United States,* p. 25.

of per capita expenses for the county as a whole; in 1970, the percentage had risen to 17. As with general government, the expenditures for protection are largely operational costs, the predominant element of which is salaries.

One might anticipate a move toward greater uniformity in expenditures for this kind of local service over time. Police and fire services seem to be particularly responsive to population growth and density; therefore, the different communities could be expected to become more like each other in their per capita protection expenditures as they become more like each other in their urban complexion. A further reason for anticipating growing similarity over time is the fact that in the 1920s and 1930s many of the county localities showed reluctance to supply their own police and fire services. Table 15 lists the coefficients of quartile variation for protection in the 16 time periods since 1925.

The table shows a trend in the last 15 years toward homo-

TABLE 15
Coefficients of Quartile Variation in
Per Capita Protection Expenditures for
Municipalities of Milwaukee County,
1925–1970

1925–1945		1950–1970	
Year	Coefficient	Year	Coefficient
1925	99	1950	81
1930	91	1952	71
1935	71	1954	78
1940	56	1956	38
1945	80	1958	37
		1960	51
		1962	36
		1964	39
		1966	34
		1968	30
		1970	34

Source: Annual Report of Clerk (Comptroller) from each locality, Municipal Audit Division, Department of Administration, State of Wisconsin.

TABLE 16
City of Milwaukee's Per Capita
Expenditures for Protection as a
Percentage of Suburban Per Capita
Expenditures, 1925–1970

1925–1945		1950–1970	
Year	Percentage	Year	Percentage
1925	269	1950	200
1930	248	1952	181
1935	209	1954	146
1940	179	1956	133
1945	179	1958	130
		1960	141
		1962	143
		1964	139
		1966	134
		1968	138
		1970	143

Source: Annual Report of the Clerk
(Comptroller) from each locality, Municipal
Audit Division, Department of Administra-
tion, State of Wisconsin.

geneity. The amount of variation in the early years is halved
in the late years. From examination of the audit reports showing how these monies are spent on protection, I would expect
this clear move toward uniformity to continue. Obviously,
there is a long way yet to go when one community is still
spending eight times as much per capita as another in 1970.
Nonetheless, this is one local service wherein urbanization
brings the communities of the metropolitan area close together
in the burdens they must bear. A similar move toward greater
uniformity was found by Burkhead.[6]

Turning to the relationship between the central city and
its suburbs, there is one item deserving of attention: the central city pays far more than its suburbs for protection. Listed
in Table 16 are the per capita amounts Milwaukee paid for

6. Burkhead, "Uniformity in Governmental Expenditures and Resources," p. 344.

police and fire protection expressed as a percentage of what
the suburbs paid. Why should it be that the central city consistently pays a good deal more per capita for police and fire
protection that its suburbs? A couple of possible reasons that
occur to mind will be tested later, namely, population density
and the age of the city. But other reasons emerge from the history of Milwaukee County. Early in this century, the city of
Milwaukee already had police and fire departments that were
winning national awards for their high quality. Its well developed fire department was a boon to the neighboring suburbs;
many of them organized little or no fire service of their own,
and depended on Milwaukee's help when fires occurred. Often
enough, Milwaukee found it difficult to collect the contract
fees from these suburbs for the fires it did fight for them.
But even if the fees were paid, the cost to the central city
was far greater than to the suburbs. Also, when some of the
suburban areas did get around to organizing their own fire
departments, they were the inexpensive volunteer type. Then,
too, many suburbs (especially towns) depended on the
county police for their protection. This obviously put an extra
burden on the central city, for in addition to supporting its
own large police force, it was supplying three-fourths and
more of the funds for the county police force, which was
acting as "local" police for many suburbs. Still another element
was the large outlay by the central city in traffic control.
That is, in addition to the traffic problems posed by the central
city's own residents, it had to cope also with the large numbers of commuters and shoppers who poured into the city
each day from the suburbs.

In addition to the higher level of protection costs in the
central city, the percentages reveal another message. There
is a long-run trend toward greater homogeneity of expenditures for this local service as between the central city and
its suburbs, which appears to have leveled out in recent time
periods.

When communities are classified by economic type, the
only consistent pattern is that industrial suburbs have regularly spent more than others for protection over the past 30

years. How about age? A plausible case can be made for predicting a relationship between the date of a municipality's incorporation and its spending on protection. The reasons are manifold. As mentioned, some of the younger communities depended for fire protection on the central city and depended for police protection on the county. Further, rural areas everywhere are much slower to provide such protective services. It also seems reasonable that older buildings would require more fire protection and older (more narrow?) streets perhaps require more traffic control. All of these influences making for higher levels of expenditures in the older communities are related to the presence or absence of "urbanization" and therefore would be expected to lessen over time.

What are the facts? The older localities do indeed, spend more for this local service, and the gap between them does, indeed, narrow over time. Thus, even though the older municipalities still spent 123 percent as much as the younger ones in 1970, this is considerably less than the 208 percent in 1960 or the 302 percent in 1940.

Therefore, in addition to both the increasing homogeneity found for the whole area and the long-run increasing homogeneity we found between the central city and its suburbs, there now also appears increasing homogeneity between the younger and the older communities. This might suggest that if one looks on functional integration as the best solution to metropolitan splintering, protection is one function whose historical trends have paved the way for countywide integration.

Regarding expenditures for protection, towns are pretty much in a class by themselves. Even as late as 1935, there was still one town (Oak Creek) showing no expenditures for protection. Further, the county's seven towns were the seven lowest spenders for protection in 1925, 1930, 1935, 1945, and at least the lowest five spenders in the other years. Thus, although towns regularly spend less for all services, their spending on protection is especially low.

Connected with this finding about towns is the matter of population density. One would imagine that higher concentration of residents raises protection costs. Brazer had expressed this same expectation and found it realized.[7] The fact that low spending towns are generally thinly settled reinforces the expectation. Rank correlations do show a significant positive relation in 1930 and 1940, but there is a decline in the correlation coefficients from then on. It turns out that the gradual emergence of high spending wealthy suburbs with low population density eliminates the correlation of the earlier years. Apparently, therefore, the relation between resources and protection expenditures outweighs and overshadows the relation between density and protection expenditures.

This last conclusion is strengthened by the rank correlation between resources and protection costs. As the correlation coefficient of density and protection costs dropped steadily in recent decades, the coefficient of resources and protection costs rose relentlessly; it shows considerably greater strength than any other.

Sanitation

For the purposes of this discussion, as in the records of the state Municipal Audit Division, sanitation includes the following: health board, sewers and sewage disposal, refuse and garbage, other health and sanitation. The relative role of sanitation in the overall spending picture tells an interesting tale over time. In 1925, sanitation accounted for 16 percent of total spending. By 1970, that had dropped to 9 percent. Clearly, there is a decline in its relative importance. Yet, those terminal figures conceal the fact that sanitation, as a share of total spending, hit its peak (18 percent) in 1954. Contrast this with police and fire protection, a function whose relative role has grown steadily during the last five decades. Moreover, protection's share of spending has been expanding in the past 15 years, a period during which sanitation's share has been declining. The conclusion appears unavoidable that each of these services grows in importance when a community or

7. Brazer, *City Expenditures*, pp. 20, 25.

region becomes urban, but in somewhat different ways. Sanitation expenditures increase while an area is going through the urbanization process and afterward decline in relative importance. Spending for protection, on the other hand, grows during the urbanization process and then grows even faster after the process is completed.

In per capita expenditures for sanitation, one feature stands out in particular. Far more than with the other two local services that have been examined, there are great leaps and jumps in sanitation costs over time as one follows the history of any individual community. And frequently one locality's expenditures for health and sanitation will be soaring upwards in the very year when its neighbor's are plummeting down. The reason for this wide variation and individuality of movement is, of course, capital outlay. This feature makes sanitation (and later, highways) quite different from the first two functions. In the case of both general government and protection, the greater part of the expenditures is listed as operating costs, whereas in the case of sanitation, a large part of the expense is capital outlay (purchase, installation, and replacement of sewers, pipes, pumps, treatment facilities, etc.) Each locality has to go through this expensive period at least once, and usually more than once, in its urbanization process. But there is no reason to expect various localities to hit this same stage of development and evolution in the same year; hence the great variations.

This brings out a large advantage and a large disadvantage of including capital outlays in the expenditure figures. On the one hand, they are so much a part of this kind of local service that an omission of them would give an unreal picture of local finances. More important, their omission would make it impossible to discern the precise time periods in which a particular municipality went through this part of the urbanization process. Simply as an example, take the last decade. Knowing that Franklin and Oak Creek were the least urbanized localities in 1960, I chose them as the ones most likely to have unusually high sanitation costs still ahead of them.

In 1960, Franklin spent $1.90 per capita on sanitation. It was still only $3.21 in 1968 (lowest in the county). Then, in 1970, the figure leaped to $91.03 per capita (triple the county average). Oak Creek was spending $3.74 per capita in 1960. The amount jumped to $43.60 in 1966 and to $60.46 in 1970. Similar illustrations can be found for each of the municipalities over the five decades. The message seems particularly useful for new local jurisdictions constantly appearing on the outer edges of the more than two hundred metropolitan areas in the United States.

The disadvantage of including capital outlays, on the other hand, is tied to the matter of timing. Capital expenditures of a particular year are normally paid for by taxpayers over a number of years; sewer bonds play a significant role in the local debt picture. Therefore, the one-year capital outlays are not matched by a corresponding tax load in that year; hence, one can not expect later figures on property tax rates to neatly match these expenditure figures.

The above references to the large role of capital spending may make one wonder about the fruitfulness of looking into the question of homogeneity. I believe, however, that small as the universe is (19 communities), it is large enough to absorb the vagaries of the individual components and still provide a meaningful picture of trends over time. The result of a search for growing uniformity appears in Table 17. The figures reveal an increase in uniformity in recent years. Examination of audit reports indicates that there is more bunching around the average since 1954, and that the trend, therefore, is likely to continue.

The central city shows considerably more stability in its sanitation expenditures than the majority of suburbs. But the question remains: which has the advantage in this matter of sanitation spending? From the point of view of age, the central city should be better off; that is, it had already constructed its sewer system, disposal plant, etc., before the period of investigation began. The central city should also have the advantage by reason of its high density (no long, open areas to connect by pipes), and in general by its ability

TABLE 17
Coefficients of Quartile Variation in
Per Capita Sanitation Expenditures for
Municipalities of Milwaukee County,
1925–1970

1925–1945		1950–1970	
Year	Coefficient	Year	Coefficient
1925	99	1950	53
1930	58	1952	48
1935	54	1954	64
1940	56	1956	60
1945	61	1958	46
		1960	41
		1962	57
		1964	44
		1966	38
		1968	33
		1970	32

Source: Annual Report of Clerk (Comptroller) from each locality, Municipal Audit Division, Department of Administration, State of Wisconsin.

to absorb new construction without great strain because of its large population. On the other hand, the central city would be at a disadvantage by reason of its annexation policy. That is, the main attraction for new areas to be annexed by Milwaukee was the desire of obtaining just such services as sanitation and of having the costs of these services shared by the older Milwaukee residents. Many of the county localities take care of their sewage needs through the Metropolitan Sewage Commission, an extension of the central city's original facilities.

Whether these two forces balance each other out is difficult to say, but the fact is that the central city and the suburban average spending per capita stay very close to one another over the 45 years for which data are available. Neither appears to have a clear advantage. And there is little opportunity for them to become more like one another over time, for they were never far apart in the first place.

There is no trend toward or away from fiscal uniformity in this local service among different economic classes. The median for the balanced type of locality is always below the suburban average, and the industrial suburbs have been spending more than others on this function since the early 1950s; otherwise there is little consistency.

When local units of government are divided into groups on the basis of their date of incorporation, it might be reasonable to expect the older localities to have the advantage. They should have already made a good start on the capital costs related to sanitation before our period begins. How wrong that expectation proves to be. From 1935 on, the median per capita expenditures of the older group is just double the median of the younger group right up to 1962. The pattern is remarkably steady, going only a little above or a little below the two to one relationship in each time period. Since 1962, however, the spending of the younger group has been drawing closer to the spending of the more established communities; in 1970, the older ones spent only 17 percent more. Thus, after considerable waiting, the anticipated move toward uniformity is finally occurring.

It would be surprising if the correlation between sanitation costs and resources were as strong as for the former two services. Apart from more frequent garbage collection, perhaps, this kind of service is not so subject to different grades of "quality." This expectation is pretty well realized. The coefficient of rank correlation hovers around the point of significance for much of the period, whereas it was always solidly significant in the case of general government and protection.

The size of the population seems to have little relation to a locality's expenditures for health and sanitation. Sometimes the coefficient of correlation is negative, sometimes it is positive, but it always remains very small. Of itself, it certainly gives no hint of economies of scale. The fact that there is regularly a positive correlation between spending on sanitation and population density also raises doubts about economies of scale.

Highways

Under this heading are included local expenditures for streets and roads, bridges, sidewalks, snow removal, and street lighting. This function had been regularly absorbing about 20 percent of total spending from the 1920s right up to 1960. Then its relative importance went into a steady decline; in 1970, it consumed only 13 percent of all expenditures. Per capita spending on highways increased in the last decade, of course, but its 35 percent growth was simply swamped by the 100 percent growth of total spending in the same 10 years.

TABLE 18
Coefficients of Quartile Variation in Per Capita Highway Expenditures for Municipalities of Milwaukee County, 1925–1970

1925–1945		1950–1970	
Year	Coefficient	Year	Coefficient
1925	18	1950	49
1930	31	1952	43
1935	57	1954	41
1940	36	1956	34
1945	42	1958	37
		1960	30
		1962	39
		1964	39
		1966	41
		1968	42
		1970	46

Source: Annual Report of Clerk (Comptroller) from each locality, Municipal Audit Division, Department of Administration, State of Wisconsin.

Table 18 lists the coefficients of quartile variation for highway spending. Over the five decades, there is no noticeable trend toward or away from increased uniformity, although there may have been a slight move away from it since the late 1950s. Therefore, in the analysis thus far, the only local function that showed a clear trend toward uniformity was protection.

The central city generally spends more for highways than the suburbs as a group. How much more Milwaukee spends is indicated by the figures in Table 19, where Milwaukee's

TABLE 19
City of Milwaukee's Per Capita Expenditures for Highways as a Percentage of Suburban Per Capita Expenditures, 1925–1970

1925–1945		1950–1970	
Year	Percentage	Year	Percentage
1925	123	1950	157
1930	110	1952	181
1935	127	1954	131
1940	139	1956	150
1945	132	1958	140
		1960	119
		1962	127
		1964	58
		1966	124
		1968	61
		1970	149

Source Annual Report of Clerk (Comptroller) from each locality, Municipal Audit Division, Department of Administration, State of Wisconsin.

per capita highway expenditures are given as a percentage of the suburban average. There is no steady move toward more or less uniformity. Yet, Milwaukee's "excess" spending on highways averages only 6 percent above its suburbs over the last decade, as compared with 52 percent in the 1950s and 26 percent in the first 20 years of the study. In this sense, it is permissible to say that the gap between them is closing. Another arresting feature of these percentages is the dramatic shift observable in 1964 and again in 1968. Over the first four decades, Milwaukee had shown unusual steadiness in its highway spending, as compared with the volatile suburbs. Individual suburbs regularly saw their per capita expenditures jump 300–400 percent in a two-year period; like sanitation, of course, this function is much influenced by capital outlays. By way of contrast, the central city (with its steadily updated seven-year capital spending program) had kept its gyrations to a minimum until the 1960s. Recently, however, its annual spending figures began jumping around, leading to the roller coaster effect in the percentages over the last five time periods.

Attempts to find factors that influence per capita spending on streets were generally disappointing. There was no significant correlation between highway spending and age, density, economic classification, or size. Resources often did show a significant correlation with highway expenditures, but the strength of the relationship did not always hold up. The connection between resources and highway expenditures may be partly blurred by heavy periodic spurts in spending due to capital expenditures.

Other Noneducational Expenditures

A few comments should be added about two categories of noneducational expenditures that are not being analyzed individually—debt payments and miscellaneous. A major difficulty with the former item is treatment of indebtedness for school purposes. In the case of cities, school debt is usually listed as part of the local debt, since the city board of education is a branch of local government. But for villages and towns, it is the individual school district and not the municipality which floats the bonds and becomes responsible for the indebtedness. This means that data listing the amount of outstanding debt, as well as data listing payments on debt, will generally include school debt for cities and will not include it for villages and towns. It is impossible, therefore, to provide an examination of indebtedness that would permit meaningful comparisons among municipalities.

Nonetheless, some findings about municipal debt in Mil-

waukee County are worth reporting. All the local units came
out of World War II in excellent condition as far as indebtedness was concerned. With all necessary cautions and qualifications made, average per capita debt payments for all the
municipalities reached their low point in 1950. Then, while
other noneducational spending was going up 103 percent
in the next 10 years, annual spending on debt went up 800
percent.

The central city regularly has had per capita debt payments
above the suburban average; this is usually the case even
when adjustment is made for educational borrowing by Milwaukee. The older localities as a group paid more for this
purpose than the younger ones.

The heading of "Miscellaneous" included such state audit
items as the following: charities, recreation (including parks),
retirement costs, judgments, damages, industrial development,
etc. Added together, these items are sometimes not negligible;
in recent years, for example, retirement costs have grown
greatly. Over most of the time periods, this category accounted for about 5 percent of total spending. The central
city has been spending about 170 percent as much as the
suburbs on this catch-all category. Older cities, in general,
show up as the heaviest spenders.

Total Noneducational Expenditures

Prior to an examination of educational expenditures, a few
words of summary and consolidation should be made about
total expenditures for noneducational services. Spending on
these municipal functions waxes and wanes with national
business conditions, even a little more than in the case of
education. In viewing the burst of per capita spending after
1945, it should be kept in mind that not only were postwar
prosperity, inflation, and population growth at work, but also
of importance was the backlog of capital projects that had
been postponed by municipalities as a contribution to the
war effort.

The decade of the 1960s manifests a modest increase in
uniformity over the 1950s in this matter of noneducational

spending, as is clear from Table 20. Howover, over the whole
45 years, no clear pattern emerges. The central city has consistently spent more than the suburbs on noneducational services. In the decade of the 1960s, Milwaukee was spending
about 10 percent more than the suburban average; this was
a smaller gap than in previous decades. To that extent, there

TABLE 20
Coefficients of Quartile Variation in
Per Capita Noneducational Expenditures
for Municipalities of Milwaukee County,
1925–1970

1925–1945		1950–1970	
Year	Coefficient	Year	Coefficient
1925	13	1950	33
1930	14	1952	50
1935	28	1954	50
1940	37	1956	41
1945	18	1958	19
		1960	19
		1962	26
		1964	28
		1966	25
		1968	27
		1970	25

Source: Annual Report of Clerk (Comp-
troller) from each locality, Municipal Audit
Division, Department of Administration,
State of Wisconsin.

is some coming together. The rather discouraging aspect, however, is that the central city continues to spend more on these
services, in spite of the fact that Milwaukee's inferior position
vis-à-vis the suburbs still remains large in nonproperty resources and has actually been worsening in property
resources.

The older municipalities had always spent more than the
younger on total noneducational services up until 1964. Since
then the two groups have stayed close to one another, with
no clear leader. Thus, there has been a real growth in homo-

geneity when local units are classified by age. This fact, plus the correlation of total noneducational spending with population density, supports the common sense expectation that demand for municipal services and the level of spending per person grow as the urbanization process advances. When noneducational expenditures are lumped together, the industrial suburbs join the central city as the big spenders. Brazer[8] came to the same conclusion as did Margolis.[9]

Of considerable interest is the relationship between population size and total nonschool expenditures—a relationship that might give a hint of economies or diseconomies of scale. This matter has intrigued many investigators. Scott and Feder found no significant correlation between the two.[10] Although Brazer felt that "both logic and our preliminary statistical analysis" [11] justified the inclusion of population size as an independent variable, yet it turned out to have no significant correlation with expenditures.[12] Similarly, Hawley found no such association in his 76 central cities,[13] nor did Hirsch in his St. Louis Metropolitan Survey.[14] The latter attempted to include in his analysis a variable measuring quality of service, and he found that, with this variable held constant, there is no association between expenditures and population size. He went further to conclude that there were few indications of economies of scale in local spending when this quality level is allowed for.

This same absence of association between population size

8. Ibid., p. 65.

9. Julius Margolis, "Municipal Fiscal Structure in a Metropolitan Region," *The Journal of Political Economy* 4 (June 1957):232.

10. Scott and Feder, *Factors Associated With Variations in Municipal Expenditure Levels*, p. 5.

11. Brazer, *City Expenditures*, p. 19.

12. Ibid., p. 25; see also p. 28 and pp. 66–67.

13. Amos H. Hawley, "Metropolitan Government and Municipal Government Expenditures in Central Cities," *Journal of Social Issues* 7 (1951):105.

14. Werner Z. Hirsch, "Expenditure Implications of Metropolitan Growth and Consolidation," *The Review of Economics and Statistics* 12 (May 1959):235.

and expenditures appears in the Milwaukee area over the last five decades. Until we have an adequate measure of quality, the question of economics of scale cannot profitably be handled. Further, even with such a measure, a multiple correlation analysis would be required in order to keep constant the variable of resources. Thus, in 1970 the three smallest populations in Milwaukee County were found in three of the wealthiest localities.

Coefficients of rank correlation show a consistent and significant correlation between resources and expenditures. In the early years, the property values taken by themselves stayed extremely close to the total resources, but as state payments became more influential, some divergence occurred. The correlation is, as we would expect, generally higher when total resources are used than it is when property resources alone are used. This strong correlation has been generally found by those in a position to test it.[15]

Existing information is not complete enough to determine whether localities spend more just because they have more to spend or whether those that have more spend more because their needs are greater. The latter influence enters into the high spending of industrial enclaves. It seems that the former influence would be likely to operate strongly in wealthy residential suburbs. In any case, the single most important determinant of noneducational spending appears to be resources.

Education

In many respects, educational expenditures are in a class by themselves. For one thing, school costs are relatively very large; generally, they are higher than the sum total of the four expenditure categories already considered. Secondly, this function is more directly and more completely dependent on the property tax than other services. Thirdly, education has

15. Scott and Feder found that this is their strongest correlation (*Factors Associated with Variations in Municipal Expenditure Levels,* p. 16), and Margolis discovered it also ("Municipal Fiscal Structure in a Metropolitan Region," p. 233).

historically had a measure of public support and political independence not matched by other local services.

The term "educational expenditures" includes the following items: payments to school treasurers, library costs, museums, vocational schools, training of handicapped children, tuition, and transportation of students. Thus, the figures used in this section will not match the item called "school district levies" on the revenue side of municipal audit reports, for this would be identical with payments to school treasurers.

In Wisconsin, the boundaries of a city are generally the boundaries of a school district. The boards of education in Wisconsin cities retain much independence even though they are in many ways part of the city administration. Outside of cities, there are only school districts, and the boundaries of these districts may or, more likely, may not coincide with those of towns and villages. The noncity school district is, therefore, an independent local unit with powers to levy taxes, vote budgets, spend money, float bonds, etc. This presents obvious difficulties in any investigation of municipal finances. One saving feature is the fact that school districts use the municipalities as their tax collection agents, and so it is possible to analyze the costs of education to any municipality. This by no means wipes out all the difficulties. The problem with school debt has already been alluded to. Also, it still remains impossible to know how many pupils come from any one locality, since records have been kept only for school districts; the presence of many different school districts in one municipality means that figures for school tax rates, per capita costs, expenditures per $1,000 of equalized property, etc., are all averages for the municipality; and finally, it is impossible to speak meaningfully of state school aids in relation to the localities being studied, since these aids go to the school district rather than to the municipality. Wisconsin ranks low in the national averages in percentage of school funds supplied by the state, but there has been some recent improvement.

The same two "halves" appear in educational spending as in spending for the first four services. That is, per capita expenditures remain remarkably constant in the first half of the study period (up to 1945), but they rise rapidly in the second half (1945–70). As has been often noted in national statistics, the postwar growth in educational spending has been considerably more rapid than the growth in local spending for nonschool purposes. Instead of using gigantic percentage rates of growth, it is perhaps easier to see the picture in terms of education's share of total local spending. In 1925, education accounted for 45 percent of total expenditures on the five services considered in this chapter. That was still about the same in 1945 (47 percent). But, by 1970, education was consuming 58 percent of total spending. Thus, the Milwaukee area manifests a pattern that is common throughout America in the postwar era; namely, school spending has been rising faster than local noneducational spending and schools, consequently, have been taking an ever greater share of property taxes.

The relative size of the postwar spurt in school spending has been greater in the suburbs than in the central city. However, as the central city staggers under the load of an eight-fold increase in per capita school spending since 1945, and the suburbs stagger under the load of an eleven-fold increase, it may seem a bootless question to ask whose knees are wobbling most.

An interesting fact emerges if one steps back for a long-range view over the past five decades. In that period the suburbs, as a group, have been increasing their per capita spending on both educational and noneducational services at a faster rate than the central city (although they still have not caught up with Milwaukee in spending on nonschool functions). Curiously, the ratios between the rates of growth are identical to the second decimal place. In both educational and in noneducational spending, Milwaukee's rate of growth is 71 percent as fast as that of the suburbs.

Do the localities of the Milwaukee area show any tendency toward growing similarity in the way they spend on education? The coefficients of quartile variation are given in Table 21. Clearly, there is no relentless trend over the whole 45

TABLE 21
Coefficients of Quartile Variation in
Per Capita Educational Expenditures for
Municipalities of Milwaukee County,
1925–1970

1925–1945		1950–1970	
Year	Coefficient	Year	Coefficient
1925	31	1950	48
1930	52	1952	39
1935	33	1954	34
1940	42	1956	30
1945	34	1958	29
		1960	33
		1962	29
		1964	36
		1966	30
		1968	32
		1970	40

Source: Annual Report of Clerk (Comptroller) from each locality, Municipal Audit Division, Department of Administration, State of Wisconsin.

years. Neither is there a recognizable movement in either direction if the focus is narrowed to the last 10 or the last 25 years.

In per capita dollar terms, there is still a six to one spread in 1970 between the municipality spending most on education and the one spending least. To the extent that dollars spent give a hint of how good the level of education is, and to the extent that educational equality is a major element in any definition of equal opportunity, this degree of disparity is disturbing. The disturbing message should, perhaps, be partially qualified by measuring how much relief or improvement the low spenders would receive if the same per capita spending pattern prevailed throughout the county. The city of St. Francis, which spends least, would see its expenditures go up from $113 per capita to $206. Naturally, most of the "equalizing" dollars would go to the city of Milwaukee, since the central city still had 68 percent of the county population in 1970. Milwaukee's spending would go up from $177 per capita to $206.

The question of homogeneity can be profitably approached also from the viewpoint of percentage shares that the localities allot to education over the years. The term "share" in this context means the percent that education is of the five expenditure categories examined in the present chapter. The coefficients of variation for these figures are shown in Table 22. It seemed reasonable to anticipate that these coefficients would be smaller in size than those for per capita spending figures. Still, the fact that they are as small as they are plus their consistency over time indicates there is considerable

TABLE 22
Coefficients of Quartile Variation in
Percentage Shares of Educational
Expenditures in Total Local Expenditures
for Municipalities of Milwaukee County,
1925–1970

1925–1945		1950–1970	
Year	Coefficient	Year	Coefficient
1925	18	1950	18
1930	11	1952	18
1935	17	1954	23
1940	18	1956	16
1945	17	1958	8
		1960	11
		1962	11
		1964	6
		1966	13
		1968	10
		1970	8

Source: Annual Report of Clerk (Comptroller) from each locality, Municipal Audit Division, Department of Administration, State of Wisconsin.

sameness within the area in the shares allocated to this function. If there is any trend at all, it is toward a little more sameness in the last decade.

To say that there has been no change in variation in percentage shares allocated to educational expenditures is, of course, not to say that the level of those percentages has stayed the same over time; it merely says that the whole metropolitan area made the same general changes in levels. As a matter of fact, the levels have edged up notably in the last 25 years.

In the light of widespread interest in the topic, I investigated with much interest the educational spending patterns of the central city as compared with its county suburbs. The main point seems to be this: the central city consistently spends less per capita on schools and also a smaller percentage of its budget for this purpose than do the suburbs. But connected with this basic fact are others: (1) the per capita difference between the central city and suburbs was quite small and stayed very steady from 1925 to 1952; (2) from the mid-1950s onward, the gap has been considerably larger; and (3) the uniqueness of the central city lies more in the percentage share of all city spending devoted to education than in its actual per capita expenditures. The central city's school portion of all spending was 43 percent in 1925, 42 percent in 1960, and 52 percent in 1970. The suburban average share devoted to education was 58 percent in 1925, 58 percent in 1960, and 66 percent in 1970. This last point means, of course, that the central city spends so much more than its suburbs on noneducational services that the share it allots to schools is far less than the suburbs' share, and was so even back in the years when the per capita figures on school spending were very similar. Even if a proportional part of Milwaukee's debt payments is allocated to schools and added on to its educational expenditures, it does very little to change the percentage relationship.

As to homogeneity, the trend has already been suggested. The small "advantage" that Milwaukee always possessed grew to about $30 or $35 per capita in the late 1950s and has leveled off since then. Whereas the suburbs as a group were spending 107 percent and 106 percent as much as Milwaukee in 1925 and in 1930, they were spending 152 percent and 151 percent as much in 1960 and 1970. There is, therefore, a distinct move away from uniformity.

The influence of "municipal overburden" has been discussed so often in the literature that treatment of it here seems unnecessary. It refers to the common belief that, because non-educational costs are so high in central cities (as compared with suburbs), proportionately fewer dollars are left to spend on education in the core city. Although the reasoning is plausible, and although spending figures in Milwaukee fit the hypothesis, it remains unproven in a cause/effect sense.

From close observation, consultation, and simple correlation analysis, it appears that the difference between the central city and the suburbs in school spending can best be explained in terms of two determinants: resources and rate of population growth. The influence of resources will be discussed shortly. As to population growth rates, the central city has been declining in population (within its 1950 borders) for at least 20 years. During the same period, the suburban population grew 44 percent, even while suburbs were losing over 20 percent of their land area. No other function offered on the local level is so directly aimed at serving people as is education. All other services are for the ultimate benefit of people, to be sure, but they generally deal directly with things (e.g., sewage, automobiles, combustible property, etc.). In education, however, human beings are not only the final beneficiaries of the service, but they are also the direct recipients. Hence the very close and direct relation between changes in population and education costs. For example, if 50 new families, each with two children, move into a locality, one cannot predict what new costs will be required for streets, sewer pipes, fire protection, etc., until it is known whether these families are all living in single homes (large or small lots?) or in duplexes or in a couple of large apartment buildings. But no matter what kind of shelter they have, one can safely predict that there is need of a new addition to the school building and of more teachers.

It is possible, of course, that there are savings connected

with the size of the central city's school system—economies of scale. It seems, however, that the influence of such economies is not great. For one thing, the lower per capita level of school spending in Milwaukee begins to assert itself only after 1952. Since it had the advantage of population size for decades before that, one wonders why the economies did not appear earlier. Further, there is no significant positive rank correlation after 1925 between population size and education costs for the municipalities of the county. In his St. Louis study, Hirsch found that there was no hint of economies of scale when he used his tentative quality variable, but he found there would be a negative correlation between size of school district and per capita school expenditures without this variable.[16]

It is truly regrettable that there is no reliable measure for quality. Certainly, common observation suggests that a better level of education is offered in most suburbs compared with large cities. This seems to be the case not only in the sense of more dollars spent and newer physical facilities, but also in the sense that the central city finds it harder to recruit and keep teachers, and in the sense that the central city has a disproportionately larger number of handicapped and underprivileged pupils.

Somewhat related to central city suburban patterns is the comparison of spending on education by older and newer jurisdictions. The older communities were spending considerably more per capita—generally about twice as much—until 1952. After that time the two groups started drawing together. In the last 15 years, they have been staying close to one another, with the younger ones spending more on education in a majority of the time periods. Why this dramatic turnabout in the 1950s? The telling reason seems to be population growth. Because of the very large number of boundary changes in the decade of the 1950s, it is necessary to measure population growth in terms of population density. It is pri-

16. Hirsch, "Expenditure Implications of Metropolitan Growth and Consolidation," p. 236.

marily the in-migration of new families that requires new schools, not the annexation of families who bring their schools with them. Since 1954 (when the change in expenditure trends started) the eight older localities show very little density growth; four of them actually declined. Of the 11 younger communities, on the other hand, eight of them increased by more than 50 percent.

Related to this matter of older and younger communities is the question of unincorporated towns. Do they have any patterns of their own? They were consistently the lowest spenders on education. In each time period the five lowest spenders were always towns, until they ceased to exist.

Turning to a different question: how do educational expenditures correlate with resources? It will be recalled that noneducational expenditures showed a stronger correlation with resources than with any other variable tested. The same is true now with educational expenditures; the coefficient is very strong—in recent years even stronger than with noneducational expenditures.

It might, perhaps, be thought odd that educational costs would correlate so strongly with a locality's resources, since it is often not the locality but the school district that decides how much to spend. However, it isn't so odd when we recall that school costs are being discussed in per capita terms. When the school district boundaries are not coterminous with local limits, the school board sets a common tax rate for all property in the district, no matter what community it is in. For River Hills (which is in three different joint school districts), this school tax rate takes a much bigger share per capita than it does from the residents of other parts of the same school district with less expensive homes. The contribution which the people of wealthy localities make to schools, is, thereby, greater per capita even though the school tax rate is the same as for their poorer neighbors in the same school district. In that light, the strong correlation between schools costs and resources is not really surprising.

The strong relation between educational expenditures and local resources does not lessen the importance assigned earlier to population growth. Resources have their effect on the level of spending, whereas population growth has its effect on relative changes in spending levels. Analysis indicates that these two forces, working simultaneously, go a long way to explain school expenditures in Milwaukee County. Thus, while some wealthy suburbs consistently spend high in per capita terms on education (influence of resources), their high level of spending still undergoes some changes (influence of population shifts).

In Table 23 are listed educational expenditures per $1,000 of equalized property valuation for each locality in each of the last six time periods. The reason for presenting school costs in this way is the fact that the local share of these costs is paid entirely from property taxes. In the case of noneducational expenditures, the relationship to equalized property valuation is of less significance, since the municipality obtains revenue for these expenditures from other sources in addition to property taxes—state income taxes, departmental earnings, special assessments, state utility taxes, etc. On rare occasions can be found a municipality with so much windfall revenue that it does not levy a local tax rate for nonschool services, and still manages to have money left over to apply to school costs; Oak Creek is an example in Milwaukee County. The new approach results in one departure from previous per capita tables: the figures did not react to general economic conditions as did per capita figures. Since property valuations moved with wars, depression, inflation, etc., and since expenditures moved with them, the parallel movement of the two keep the relationship between them constant.

And, yet, the term "constancy" could be a seriously misleading label for this set of figures. To be sure, there is constancy in the sense of being insensitive to national business cycles. Also, there is constancy in the educational spending figures per $1,000 of property values up to 1956. In that year, school expenditures per $1,000 of property were just about at the same level for the whole county as they had been 30 years earlier—$10.67. But then constancy disappeared. In the face

TABLE 23
Educational Expenditures per $1,000 Equalized Property Valuation in Municipalities of Milwaukee County, 1960–1970

	1960	1962	1964	1966	1968	1970
Milwaukee	$14.43	$17.01	$20.13	$21.34	$22.82	$25.24
Bayside	15.54	15.99	17.68	16.84	19.52	21.66
Brown Deer	14.24	20.72	18.29	16.70	17.49	18.03
Cudahy	12.24	17.79	40.97	15.98	18.14	32.28
Fox Point	16.81	15.87	17.16	16.84	20.22	21.94
Franklin	17.14	24.27	22.50	22.04	22.19	21.14
Glendale	9.66	9.88	13.63	12.99	14.85	33.68
Greendale	11.33	14.79	18.21	16.12	17.92	16.98
Greenfield	18.15	19.23	19.09	18.87	17.85	18.24
Hales Corners	17.98	20.08	20.47	20.74	20.32	20.08
Oak Creek	35.23	36.13	28.54	30.87	33.50	35.39
River Hills	13.91	14.33	14.15	15.35	19.21	24.08
St. Francis	15.66	16.95	19.77	19.66	18.94	20.76
Shorewood	14.70	16.05	16.75	17.46	18.45	18.92
S. Milwaukee	21.93	19.39	22.42	21.79	26.13	22.80
Wauwatosa	15.15	11.99	12.78	15.04	19.96	17.36
W. Allis	17.93	17.76	21.62	20.87	23.02	36.26
W. Milwaukee	8.62	9.63	11.13	10.92	11.83	15.43
Whitefish Bay	15.49	16.18	18.21	18.77	20.51	22.45
Suburbs Only	15.96	16.17	19.18	17.78	20.37	25.21
Entire County	14.97	16.74	19.79	19.96	21.83	25.23

Sources: for expenditure data, Annual Report of Clerk (Comptroller) from each locali y, Municipal Audit Division, Department of Administration, State of Wisconsin; for property valuations, Assessors of Incomes Statistical Report of Property Valuations for the County of Milwaukee, Office of Tax Commission, State of Wisconsin.

of the World War II baby boom and of higher costs per pupil, educational expenditures per $1,000 of property have more than doubled in the past 15 years. Although interesting comparisons and divergences will later be pointed out between the central city and suburbs, between old and new municipalities, etc., these observations should not obscure the fact that all communities in Milwaukee County have been swept along by the strong winds of change. The change is this: property values and school spending moved together in the 1920s, 1930s, 1940s, and part of the 1950s; since 1956 however, school spending has increased much faster than the property tax base supporting it. Thus, as per capita property base increased 66 percent in the county over the last 15 years, per capita educational expenditures increased 293 percent.

In Table 24 are listed the coefficients of variation in school expenditures per $1,000 of property over the last 45 years. The most striking feature of the table is the consistency with

TABLE 24
Coefficients of Quartile Variation in
Educational Expenditures per $1,000 of
Equalized Property Valuation for
Municipalities of Milwaukee County,
1925–1970

1925–1945		1950–1970	
Year	Coefficient	Year	Coefficient
1925	38	1950	30
1930	49	1952	27
1935	55	1954	27
1940	44	1956	18
1945	34	1958	17
		1960	13
		1962	10
		1964	13
		1966	13
		1968	11
		1970	16

Sources: for expenditure data, Annual Report of Clerk (Comptroller) from each locality, Municipal Audit Division, Department of Administration, State of Wisconsin; for property valuations, Assessors of Incomes Statistical Report of Property Valuations for the County of Milwaukee, Office of Tax Commission, State of Wisconsin.

which the localities are coming closer and closer together
in the way they match their school expenditures to their resources. The average variation of the first 25 years is halved
during the 1950s and almost halved again during the 1960s.
Of course, this is not to deny that there are great differences
among the localities in per capita school expenditures (and
presumably, therefore, in eduational quality.)

Examination of the coefficient computations shows that this
impressive growth of homogeneity results from the fact that
the lower-spending communities raised their ratio of spending to property values much faster than the higher-spending
ones. Right into the mid-1950s the upper quartile was at just
about the same ratio between spending and resources as it
had been 25 and 30 years earlier; but over that same period
the bottom quartile had been steadily spending more and
more in relation to its property base. Whether this march toward uniformity be the result of greater general concern for
educational standards, or the result of pressure from the state
capital, or the result of redistribution of population, or other
factors is beyond the scope of this study to say. But there is
much value in knowing that such is the case, whatever be the
causal influences.

Our findings about the relation between educational expenditures and property values are a contribution to any discussion of "the metropolitan problem." Education is widely recognized as a public service whose benefits spill over a whole
nation, or at least over a whole state, or, at the very least,
over a whole county. Yet, the economic base that supports
this service is splintered up not only into numerous municipalities, but into even smaller units—school districts. The
findings of this chapter tell us that communities are coming
closer and closer to one another over time in the burden
that schools put on the property tax base. The amounts the
municipalities spend per capita, on the other hand, are not
coming closer together; recall the enormous six to one spread
still existing in 1970. The foregoing contrast contains a message. Countywide fiscal support of education is called for
by the economic unity of the entire area; it is called for by

the indirect benefits (spillovers) inherent in education; it is called for by the need for equal opportunity in a democracy.[17] This study shows that the relentless move of history has brought the municipalities so close together in their relations between school costs and tax base that countywide fiscal support of education would cause very little change in anybody's school tax rates. Nonetheless, if Milwaukee County took the last step along the road prepared by history, it would do away with very large discrepancies in per capita spending and in educational quality.

Granted that variation in Table 24 is lessening, it is still true, nevertheless, that some differences remain. In general, which kinds of localities have higher expenditures per $1,000 of property? The central city always spent more in relation to its property base than the average of its suburbs—at least until 1956. In the last 15 years, they spent about the same amount in relation to property tax base. It is clear that a measure of caution is called for in speaking of "advantage" or "burden" in the matter of local spending, for Milwaukee always spent less per capita than the suburban average, but nearly always spent more per $1,000 of tax base than the suburbs.

One interesting question about the relation of school spending to property resources is whether the wealthier localities pay more or less than average. In general, they pay less per $1,000 than those not so wealthy. The correlations between property resources and school expenditures per $1,000 of property are always negative, but rarely is the correlation strong enough to be statistically significant. But for the very wealthy (the highest three or four localities), there is great consistency in the way in which they hug the bottom of the rankings in terms of educational expenditures per $1,000.

17. The point about equal opportunity in a democracy is not simply an expression of my personal preference. During the years 1971 and 1972 separate court cases have ruled that present financing of education in at least five states is unconstitutional because dependence on local property taxes provides more money for educating children in wealthy districts than for educating children in poor districts.

Connected with this finding is another interesting point. Over the decades, towns were almost always in the bottom half of the rankings in terms of school expenditures per $1,000 of equalized property valuation. Thus, the lower spenders (under this definition) were a strange mixture of unincorporated towns and very wealthy suburbs. Obviously, they did not share this lower part of the rankings for the same reasons. It seems that the wealthy suburbs spent less simply because they were so wealthy; this is especially true of education, where the property value supplies the revenue and the population size determines the costs. But why were towns also consistently low spenders per $1,000? The reasons here are not so obvious. The traditional simplicity of educational service offered by rural areas in bygone days apparently goes far to explain it. In any case, up to about 1950, towns in the state of Wisconsin regularly had lower school tax rates than cities and villages. Since then, the towns have been averaging as much or more than incorporated localities.

Since expenditures per capita and expenditures per $1,000 of property tax base often go off in different directions, behave in different ways, and fall on the same locality with different effects, the question arises: which of the two is the more significant measure of tax burden? By talking just about school costs, we have abstracted from the matter of returned taxes from the state. "Returned taxes from the state" means the same thing as the "shared taxes" discussed in Chapter 5. These funds are used by municipalities for noneducational expenditures. We do not have to worry that the present question about burden may be distorted by these very uneven amounts of shared taxes, for shared taxes are not used to pay school expenditures.

The more significant measure of burden for school costs would seem to be the amount spent per $1,000 of property valuation. It is true that the actual amount paid out by each taxpayer (the per capita figure) certainly has a very personal significance to him. Yet, any meaningful discussion of "burden" must be in terms of ability to pay. The ratio of expenditures to available tax base is, therefore, more revealing. In terms of this ratio, (1) the central city always had a higher burden than its suburbs up until 1956, while since then the suburban average has been much closer; (2) the towns had a lighter burden than the incorporated localities; (3) the wealthier suburbs have regularly had a lighter burden than the rest.

Total Per Capita Expenditures

It is time to put together the two halves of local spending: educational and noneducational expenditures. The word "total" claims, perhaps, too much. Only the five services previously examined in detail are included in the total; namely, general government, protection, sanitation, highways, and education.

A feel for the magnitudes involved can be gained from Table 25, which covers the last six of the study's 17 time periods. After looking at the "Entire County" figure of $357.55

TABLE 25
Total Per Capita Expenditures of Municipalities in Milwaukee County, 1960–1970

	1960	1962	1964	1966	1968	1970
Milwaukee	$176.05	$192.26	$191.12	$250.46	$269.28	$336.58
Bayside	243.65	254.41	275.13	382.70	343 65	414.47
Brown Deer	143.44	150.73	165.70	195.61	219.06	259.15
Cudahy	153.44	193.94	374.82	225.07	234.83	447.59
Fox Point	262.20	268.57	279.38	296.96	346.33	427.67
Franklin	102.90	133.20	133.43	149.89	162.97	308.68
Glendale	230.99	237.85	361.52	366.38	393.54	837.96
Greendale	159.87	125.85	148.12	183.04	211.46	229.89
Greenfield	111.47	116.66	137.78	219.85	333.55	326.33
Hales Corners	238.24	171.05	208.72	229.78	232.76	278.54
Oak Creek	329.29	376.68	383.74	476.83	605.15	647.32
River Hills	443.92	453.15	473.74	539.06	632.43	786.09
St. Francis	95.08	135.39	143.23	175.91	163.21	200.46
Shorewood	161.03	173.77	186.28	213.56	250.12	277.81
S. Milwaukee	203.27	170.79	199.68	192.88	240.24	245.07
Wauwatosa	188.16	178.75	178.96	230.28	334.97	318.54
W. Allis	227.15	234.62	276.68	282.43	347.28	514.56
W. Milwaukee	431.88	475.96	571.51	600.55	757.58	1,059.07
Whitefish Bay	184.95	190.80	200.15	220.16	255.53	331.15
Suburbs Only	196.27	200.75	233.83	253.84	314.75	402.15
Entire County	181.72	194.73	203.86	251.50	283.46	357.55

Source: Annual Report of Clerk (Comptroller) for each locality, Municipal Audit Division, Department of Administration, State of Wisconsin.

for 1970, it is difficult to realize that the corresponding figure was only $54.95 in 1930, $45.71 in 1940, and $89.58 in 1950. The decade covered by Table 25 (1960s) saw education's share of the five services for the whole county grow from 46 percent to 58 percent.

The central city always had a higher total spending figure than the suburban average until 1956; since then, Milwaukee has been spending relatively less. In the vast majority of the 16 time periods for which data are available, the difference never exceeded 15 percent either way. It is education that explains the change in the mid-1950s; Milwaukee still spends more than the suburbs on noneducational services.

A look at the wide spread between the biggest spender and smallest spender reveals that much variation remains among the 19 localities. In 1970, the spread was five to one. Even if an attempt is made to remove the extremes by lopping off the two at the top and the two at the bottom, the spread is still an impressive three to one. Has this much variation in spending pattern always characterized the municipalities of Milwaukee County? As a matter of fact, the variation was worse more often than not over the last five decades. Coefficients of quartile variation are presented in Table 26.

If any trend is visible at all in Table 26, there is a modest increase in uniformity during the decade of the 1960s as compared with the decade of the 1950s. This growing homogeneity of expenditure patterns takes on considerable significance when it is contrasted with the earlier findings of little or no change in homogeneity in property values and the finding of lessening homogeneity in state payments (especially the shared income tax). If the municipalities are becoming a little more like one another in their spending of money and a little less like one another in their ability to raise money, then "the metropolitan problem" shows signs of worsening. In other words, the economic unity that is the heart of a metropolitan area impels all the parts to act alike in providing urban services (the expenditures side). But the governmental splintering that turns a metropolitan area into a metropolitan problem permits each splinter to claim the resources that happen

TABLE 26
Coefficients of Quartile Variation in Total
Per Capita Expenditures for Municipalities
of Milwaukee County, 1925–1970

1925–1945		1950–1970	
Year	Coefficient	Year	Coefficient
1925	24	1950	43
1930	24	1952	36
1935	31	1954	38
1940	35	1956	37
1945	32	1958	18
		1960	23
		1962	16
		1964	37
		1966	30
		1968	20
		1970	30

Source: Annual Report of Clerk (Comp-
troller) from each locality, Municipal Audit
Division, Department of Administration,
State of Wisconsin.

to end up within its borders. The present investigation indicates that the resources are becoming more unevenly apportioned over time, even though the pressures of metropoli-
tanization, as reflected in expenditure patterns, are becoming
more even over time. The outlook is not reassuring.

The great surge in total spending over the past 20 years
(299 percent) is neatly matched by a comparable surge in
total resources (330 percent). And, yet, how misleading is
the comfortable picture those totals suggest! Actually, the two
major components of spending acted quite differently from
one another. Educational spending has grown 338 percent
between 1950 and 1970; noneducational spending has grown
188 percent—a little better than half as much. That is only
part of the picture. On the resource side, property values
have increased 173 percent in the last 20 years, whereas state
payments have grown 437 percent. Thus the property base

has grown at a relatively slow pace, whereas the function it primarily supports—education—has grown at a rapid rate. State payments, on the other hand, have grown impressively, whereas the functions they primarily support—noneducational services—have grown at a moderate rate. This suggests very persuasively that school tax rates have probably risen greatly, while local (municipal) tax rates have probably risen much more modestly, or perhaps even declined. Chapter 7 demonstrates that these high probabilities are, as a matter of fact, actualities.

7 Property Tax Rates

FIRST, it will be useful to look at the property tax rates of the Milwaukee metropolitan area and see how they have behaved over the past five decades; and then an attempt will be made to interpret that behavior. Of background value for the present investigation are two findings from an earlier study that embraced the whole state of Wisconsin. "Wisconsin property taxes as a percentage of personal income, while still below the peaks reached in 1932, have increased 60 percent during the postwar period. Property taxes have increased 5 percent faster than full value assessments, but construction costs and presumably prices entering into property values have increased 22 percent more rapidly than prices in general."[1] Regarding the first point, the rise of property taxes as a percentage of income since 1946 is especially striking in view of the great growth of personal income during this same period. As to the second point, Knight estimated the effect of this relatively greater increase of property and construction costs on full value tax rates. He concluded that when rates are adjusted for this factor, they increased 99 percent from 1929 to 1960 and increased 28 percent between 1946 and 1960.[2]

1. W. D. Knight, *Property Taxation and the Wisconsin Tax System* (Madison: University of Wisconsin Bureau of Business Research and Service, 1960), p. 57.
2. Ibid., p. 23.

Behavior of Tax Rates

Since there are no independent special districts with the power to levy property taxes in Milwaukee County, the present discussion deals with five property tax rates:

1. *Local Rate:* The rate imposed by a municipality to raise funds for supporting the noneducational services it provides its citizens. Such services are police and fire protection, courts, sewage and rubbish disposal, street construction and maintenance, recreation, etc. It is important to remember that unincorporated jurisdictions (towns) are classified as municipalities in Wisconsin.

2. *School Rate:* The rate determined by the local school board for maintaining educational services. Although school district boundaries often differ from municipal boundaries, it is possible to determine a school rate for each municipality.

3. *County Rate:* The rate determined by the county government to provide funds for the support of such services as welfare, roads, the sheriffs' department, county courts, board of health, institutional care, etc.

4. *Total Rate:* The sum of local, school, and county rates, plus a negligible amount of state property taxes (averaging only 0.2 of one mill).

5. *"Effective" Total Rate:* Since 1962 the state of Wisconsin has been giving funds to local governments which must be used to reduce property tax rates. The effective rate is the total rate that remains after the property tax credit portion has been subtracted from the total rate.

It is crucial to keep in mind that the entire discussion of property tax rates is in terms of full value rates, or market value rates, or equalized rates. This is what makes comparisons valid and useful. Each local government in Wisconsin assesses property for tax purposes and, to the dismay of many, each municipality has its own peculiar way of assessing property at 30 percent of its market value, or 75 percent, or whatever. To compare rates based on these assessed values would be worse than useless; it would be positively misleading. Wisconsin's well-developed system of reappraising all the property by state assessors provides another set of values based on 100 percent of the sale value of the parcel—hence the terms "market value" and "full value." When tax rates are translated into these uniformly assessed property values, full value tax rates emerge which are truly capable of being honestly compared. The source of information, therefore, for the data underlying this chapter is the Wisconsin Department of Revenue, Bureau of Property Taxation. It produces annual bulletins, which give tax rate information by county.

Table 27 lists the local, school, and two kinds of total rates for Milwaukee County localities over the past decade.[3] It is best to begin our analysis with the total rates. The significance of this set of rates is obvious: when a taxpayer speaks of his property taxes (more often than not in a bitter tone), it is to this total rate that he refers. For most people, it matters not whether one or six governments are taxing his property; the total bite, however, definitely does matter. By 1970, the total rates ranged from 30.6 mills (or $30.60 per $1,000 of true value) in Oak Creek to 48.3 mills in the city of Milwaukee. In 1970 the rates were at their 50-year peak. Up until the mid-1960s, however, the previous top rates had been recorded around the end of the Great Depression. When the collapsed property values of the 1930s are compared with the inflated property values of 1970, it is perhaps understandable that some see signs of urban fiscal crisis in the fact that 1970 rates still manage to exceed the depression era property tax rates. Perhaps the most impressive fact about total tax rates is their enormous rise since the mid-1950s. In the last 15 years, total rates throughout the county increased more than 70 percent. Thus, although some municipalities bear much heavier burdens than others and although sizeable fiscal disparities exist, these considerations should

3. Data on earlier years is available in Donald J. Curran, "The Financial Evolution of the Milwaukee Metropolitan Area" (Ph.D. Diss., University of Wisconsin, 1963).

not distract us from the fact that all jurisdictions have seen their total tax rates rise dramatically in recent years.

The local rates generally follow the movements of the total rates. One exception is that the local rate for a majority of the localities reached its peak in 1935. This was partly the result of a transfer of some local functions to the county level during the late 1930s (causing both a drop in the local rate and a jump of more than 100 percent in the county tax rate). The drop in the local rates was also the result of notable growth in the amount of shared taxes from the state. Since these funds are used for municipal purposes, rather than school or county purposes, they took pressure off local tax rates for a majority of municipalities. In any case, most local rates have constituted a considerably smaller percentage of total rates in the last half of our 50 years than they did in the first half.

The school rates move in a general way with the total rates. In the light of Chapter 6, we would expect school tax rates to have risen more quickly than others since 1945. This expectation is fulfilled. The trend is even more dramatically reflected in the relative share of total property taxes which go to local and to school purposes. Thus, whereas the school rate for the suburbs was 144 percent as large as the local rate in 1945, it was 384 percent as large in 1970.

It may come as a surprise to some that county tax rates have increased most of all. They have more than quadrupled over the past 50 years. The main reason is that the county is doing many more things than it used to do; it has taken on proportionately more new responsibilities than either the school district or the municipality. This trend harmonizes well with the growing economic unity and economic interdependence of the metropolitan area. Many students of the metropolitan problem, having long since abandoned the crusade for areawide government, are heartened by the occasional transfer of functions from municipalities to counties as a second-best solution.

The effective total rates have a short history. With the minimum threshhold of eligibility for relief set low (14 mills),

TABLE 27
Property Tax Rates of Municipalities in Milwaukee County, 1960–1970

| | 1960 | | | | 1962 | | | |
	Local	School	Total[a]	Effec.[b] Total	Local	School	Total[a]	Effec. Total
Milwaukee	11.3	11.5	31.9		13.1	12.8	35.6	31.3
Bayside	0.7	15.6	25.4		0.7	16.0	26.5	23.6
Brown Deer	2.4	15.8	27.5		2.6	16.4	28.9	25.6
Cudahy	6.9	10.5	26.5		6.4	11.6	27.6	24.7
Fox Point	0.8	16.2	26.3		0.8	16.7	27.3	24.3
Franklin	0.4	19.5	29.2		1.6	25.2	36.6	32.9
Glendale	0.6	9.5	19.4		0.6	11.1	21.4	19.7
Greendale	2.2	15.9	26.4		2.2	17.7	29.8	26.3
Greenfield	0.5	20.0	29.9		1.8	19.9	31.6	27.8
Hales Corners	0.5	18.5	28.4		1.3	20.4	31.5	27.6
Oak Creek	0.1	15.6	22.6		0.0	15.2	22.3	20.4
River Hills	0.1	15.3	24.8		0.5	14.5	24.8	22.1
St. Francis	2.3	17.6	29.3		2.8	24.3	37.0	33.0
Shorewood	4.1	14.5	27.9		4.6	15.0	29.4	26.2
S. Milwaukee	8.7	11.4	28.2		8.8	15.1	32.4	29.0
Wauwatosa	2.3	12.0	23.5		3.2	12.2	25.0	22.7
W. Allis	8.8	10.5	28.4		10.9	10.9	31.5	28.0
W. Milwaukee	1.4	9.7	20.2		3.3	9.7	22.6	21.0
Whitefish Bay	0.8	15.4	25.5		1.1	16.0	27.0	25.9
Suburbs Only	3.9	12.7	25.7		4.7	13.6	27.8	
Entire County	8.8	12.0	29.9		10.1	13.1	32.8	

| | 1964 | | | | 1966 | | | |
	Local	School	Total[a]	Effec. Total	Local	School	Total[a]	Effec. Total
Milwaukee	12.9	15.4	38.9	35.1	13.8	16.5	40.7	36.8
Bayside	2.1	17.1	29.9	27.7	0.2	18.3	30.8	28.5
Brown Deer	2.1	19.2	32.0	28.8	2.4	20.3	33.1	29.9
Cudahy	5.9	13.7	30.2	27.7	3.4	16.8	30.6	28.2
Fox Point	1.4	17.7	29.8	27.5	0.9	18.9	30.1	27.9
Franklin	0.4	23.8	34.9	31.5	1.5	22.2	34.1	31.0
Glendale	0.2	12.2	23.0	20.8	0.7	13.0	24.1	22.3
Greendale	2.1	18.8	31.6	27.8	2.4	19.3	32.1	28.5
Greenfield	2.2	20.0	32.8	29.7	0.6	20.6	31.6	27.8
Hales Corners	1.3	20.6	32.6	28.9	2.2	20.9	33.5	30.3
Oak Creek	0.0	15.4	23.1	21.3	0.0	20.1	23.0	21.0
River Hills	1.9	15.7	28.3	26.4	2.5	16.8	29.7	27.6
St. Francis	3.5	19.8	34.0	30.7	5.6	19.8	35.8	32.9
Shorewood	5.7	16.2	32.6	30.0	5.4	17.1	32.9	30.2
S. Milwaukee	6.6	16.8	32.7	29.4	4.9	19.1	32.2	29.1
Wauwatosa	3.5	12.7	26.8	24.7	3.4	12.5	26.3	24.1
W. Allis	10.7	11.6	32.9	29.6	10.1	12.1	32.6	29.5
W. Milwaukee	3.3	11.4	25.3	23.7	3.3	11.9	25.6	24.0
Whitefish Bay	1.7	18.1	30.5	28.2	1.6	19.7	31.7	29.3
Suburbs Only	4.7	14.5	29.6		4.2	15.4	29.6	
Entire County	9.8	15.0	35.4		0.1	16.1	36.4	

(Table continued on next page)

TABLE 27 (continued)

| | 1968 | | | | 1970 | | | |
	Local	School	Total[a]	Effec. Total	Local	School	Total[a]	Effec. Total
Milwaukee	14.7	20.9	47.4	43.8	15.3	20.8	48.3	45.0
Bayside	2.1	22.2	36.1	33.6	1.7	23.3	37.2	35.0
Brown Deer	4.0	20.0	35.8	33.0	3.0	24.0	39.2	36.8
Cudahy	3.7	20.0	35.6	33.5	6.2	22.2	40.6	38.5
Fox Point	0.9	23.0	35.7	33.6	0.1	24.7	37.8	35.8
Franklin	2.6	23.5	37.9	34.7	2.7	24.0	38.9	36.2
Glendale	0.8	14.7	27.3	25.8	1.6	17.0	30.8	29.4
Greendale	3.3	21.2	36.3	32.7	2.8	22.8	37.7	34.9
Greenfield	2.0	20.3	34.1	30.1	2.6	21.3	36.1	32.9
Hales Corners	2.8	22.1	36.8	34.1	2.4	23.9	38.5	36.2
Oak Creek	0.0	19.9	28.1	26.3	0.1	21.6	30.6	28.8
River Hills	2.5	20.9	35.2	33.1	2.3	21.3	35.7	33.6
St. Francis	6.0	20.4	38.2	35.5	6.5	22.4	41.1	38.7
Shorewood	6.3	18.3	36.5	34.1	6.2	21.9	40.3	38.1
S. Milwaukee	5.6	19.5	35.7	33.1	6.3	21.4	38.8	36.5
Wauwatosa	3.3	15.0	30.1	28.4	3.2	16.6	32.0	30.4
W. Allis	9.5	14.1	35.4	32.8	10.0	15.0	36.1	33.8
W. Milwaukee	5.1	14.3	31.2	29.8	7.0	15.9	35.0	33.4
Whitefish Bay	2.5	21.5	35.7	33.5	2.3	24.5	39.1	36.9
Suburbs Only	4.4	17.3	33.3		5.0	19.1	35.7	
Entire County	10.6	19.5	41.7	38.7[c]	11.0	20.2	43.1	40.2[c]

Source: *Town, Village and City Taxes,* annual bulletins published by the Department of Revenue, State of Wisconsin.

[a] To determine the county tax rate, subtract local and school rates from this total. With very minor exceptions, the county tax rate is the same for all jurisdictions within the county.

[b] Property tax relief, which gives rise to the Effective Total Rate, was inaugurated in 1961.

[c] The annual bulletins first provided an average Effective Total Rate for the entire county in 1968.

each municipality in Milwaukee County receives funds. The most relief in millage terms was received by the city of Milwaukee in 1970 (equivalent to 3.3 mills); the least was received by Glendale (1.4 mills). The credit clearly did little to bridge the gap of 18 mills in the total tax rates of these two neighbors. It was observed in Chapter 5 that when the credit is expressed in per capita dollar terms, the communities with the richest per capita property base receive the most.

How about growing uniformity of tax rates over the years? This is the central question of the whole study. Its importance in this matter of tax rates is enhanced by reason of the grip that tax rates have on citizens' emotions. The quartile coefficients of variation for total rates are offered in Table 28. The movement toward increasing uniformity is very striking.

TABLE 28
Coefficients of Quartile Variation in Total
Property Tax Rates for Municipalities of
Milwaukee County, 1925–1970

| 1925–1945 | | 1950–1970 | |
Year	Coefficient	Year	Coefficient
1925	36.5	1950	12.1
1930	37.0	1952	7.2
1935	33.8	1954	7.7
1940	17.7	1956	9.8
1945	18.3	1958	9.6
		1960	6.8
		1962	11.7
		1964	7.4
		1966	5.4
		1968	3.4
		1970	5.7

Sources: Table 27, and Donald J. Curran,
"The Financial Evolution of the Milwaukee
Metropolitan Area" (Ph. D. Diss., Univer-
sity of Wisconsin, 1963), pp. 244–46.

A galaxy of interesting and persuasive explanations spring
to mind. But most of them fail to stand up under this fact:
the increase in tax rate uniformity is not accompanied by
a parallel uniformity in the major determinants of tax rates—
resources and expenditures.

The explanation based on historical analysis is a simple
one. Rapid population growth in the low-spending communities sent their school tax rates shooting upward; the older
communities, however, who were already "big spenders" in
tax rate terms had no such explosive population growth and,
therefore, experienced a more restrained tax rate increase.
The result was a coming together of the two groups and
greater similarity in the entire tax rate picture. The trend
was strengthened by the growing county share in the total
rate; since the county rate is the same for all, its relative
expansion guaranteed an increase in uniformity.

Is the impressive increase of homogeneity in total tax rates
matched by a corresponding movement in local tax rates?
The answer is a negative one. The 1960s manifest somewhat
more similarity than the 1950s, but far less similarity than
the early decades. The quartile coefficients of variation are
listed in Table 29. It would be a mistake to read too much
significance into the modest increase in similarity in 1968 and
1970. Even in 1970 one county jurisdiction had a local tax
rate 150 times as big as another; there were ten communities
with local rates of less than three mills, while two of the
communities had rates of ten and 15 mills; and the central
city had a local tax rate three times as large as the suburban
average—a relationship that has been generally true for the
past 25 years.

Common sense expectations are borne out when relative
wealth of property tax base is used as an explanatory factor

TABLE 29
**Coefficients of Quartile Variation in Local
Property Tax Rates for Municipalities of
Milwaukee County, 1925-1970**

1925–1945		1950–1970	
Year	Coefficient	Year	Coefficient
1925	63.9	1950	51.5
1930	46.2	1952	70.5
1935	31.8	1954	74.1
1940	31.5	1956	65.5
1945	35.8	1958	78.9
		1960	78.3
		1962	70.4
		1964	60.6
		1966	69.0
		1968	38.3
		1970	45.9

Source: Table 27, and Donald J. Curran,
"The Financial Evolution of the Milwaukee
Metropolitan Area" (Ph. D. Diss., Univer-
sity of Wisconsin, 1963), pp. 244–46.

for the widely different local tax rates. In 1970, for example, the five municipalities with the lowest rates are all in the top six municipalities ranked by per capita property valuation. Inasmuch as property values and state payments go so well together, low local rates are also closely associated with high payments from the state capital.

Older, balanced communities generally have the highest local tax rates. Although there are many plausible reasons for this, it is not perfectly clear which factors are dominant. In any case, it is important and valuable to know that it is a fact, especially in view of the other fiscal disadvantages experienced by balanced communities.

Since the total tax rates have grown so impressively similar, and since local rates have failed to do so, it would hardly be surprising to find that school rates have drawn closer together. They have. Table 30 gives the coefficients of variation

TABLE 30
Coefficients of Quartile Variation in School Tax Rates for Municipalities of Milwaukee County, 1925–1970

1925–1945		1950–1970	
Year	Coefficient	Year	Coefficient
1925	26.9	1950	8.1
1930	50.4	1952	15.0
1935	48.2	1954	15.5
1940	48.2	1956	17.5
1945	28.3	1958	22.9
		1960	17.4
		1962	18.4
		1964	16.7
		1966	9.8
		1968	7.3
		1970	6.9

Source: Table 27, and Donald J. Curran, "The Financial Evolution of the Milwaukee Metropolitan Area" (Ph. D. Diss., University of Wisconsin, 1963), pp. 244–46.

for these school rates. The actual millage increase in the size
of school tax rates in recent years almost takes the breath
away. For example, in the single decade 1958–68 the average
school rate in the county just about doubled, rising from 10.7
mills to 19.5 mills. Although students of taxation have known
for years that it is education which caused the fantastic rise
in property taxes around the nation in the last 25 years, many
ordinary taxpayers seem much less aware of this fact. In the
Milwaukee area, this notable increase in school tax rates was
accompanied by an actual decline in local tax rates in a majority of municipalities; whether this pattern is true in most
metropolitan areas of the United States is a question worth
pursuing. It may bring greater clarity and focus to the re-
peated rumblings about the "taxpayer revolt."

A comparison of the central city with its suburbs in terms
of tax rates is quite revealing. Having seen that the central
city is worse off than its suburbs both in property tax base
and in state payments, and knowing that the central city
spends more per capita on most local services, we are prepared to find Milwaukee's tax rates higher. Such is the case.
Listed in Table 31 are Milwaukee's rates as a percentage
of the suburban average rate for each of the time periods.

The central city is at a monumental disadvantage in its
local rate, and its position has grown considerably worse in
the last two decades. In school rates the central city used
to have an advantage, but that has disappeared since the
early 1960s; in the last four time periods, the central city
has had, on the average, school tax rates 10 percent above
the suburbs. When Milwaukee's bleak position in local rates
is added to its bleak position in school rates, the total rate
picture is, predictably, not a bright one. In the late 1950s,
it appeared that Milwaukee had settled into a consistent pattern of total tax rates that were one-fourth higher than the
suburbs taken as a group. That was bad enough, but the
decade of the 1960s has seen the disparity grow still worse.

As far as trends toward uniformity are concerned, the last
25 years show a movement away from uniformity between
the central city and its suburbs in the matter of local rates.

TABLE 31
Milwaukee's Tax Rates as a Percentage of the Suburban Average Rates, 1925–1970

Year	Local	School	Total[a]
1925	217	88	135
1930	225	108	143
1935	152	108	124
1940	211	97	128
1945	221	110	136
1950	305	98	132
1952	306	88	127
1954	314	88	124
1956	320	87	125
1958	315	86	124
1960	290	91	124
1962	280	94	128
1964	274	103	131
1966	379	107	138
1968	334	121	142
1970	306	109	135

Source: Table 27, and Donald J. Curran, "The Financial Evolution of the Milwaukee Metropolitan Area" (Ph. D. Diss., University of Wisconsin, 1963), pp. 244–46.

[a] This is the sum of local, school, and county taxes; it does not include adjustment for property tax relief.

In school rates, the gap between the central city and the rest of the county was about the same size in the late 1960s as it had been in the 1950s; the only difference is that the gap is now against Milwaukee instead of in its favor. In total rates, exclusive of the property tax credit, there is an increase in the central city's disadvantage in the later years, and, to that extent, a lessening of uniformity. One commentator wrote in 1958 with reference to the previous ten years, "The gap between the tax rates in the suburbs and City of Milwaukee is closing rapidly."[4] His remark, while true of the decade he referred to, would certainly mislead anyone who understood the use of the present tense to imply that the closing of the gap was destined to continue.

Simple observation of Table 27 suggests a number of relationships when the county localities are divided up according to date of incorporation. The information on this point appears in Figure 2. The topmost point of each bar is the median total tax rate for the respective groups; the upper part of each bar represents local rates, then come school rates, and finally the open space at the bottom represents county and state rates. Figure 2 tells an interesting tale, which can be summarized thus:

1. The older localities always have significantly higher local rates.

2. In school rates, the new localities took the lead in 1952 and have kept it since. The gap widened in the 1950s, but then narrowed in the 1960s.

3. The force of this surging school rate in the newer localities has so outweighed their advantage in local rates that their total rates have steadily gained on the older group. As the study period ends (1970), the older communities, however, still have a modestly higher total rate.

When the localities are grouped according to economic type, there is little consistency in the movements of tax rates. What does show up is a tendency in recent years for residential localities to have the lowest local rates and for industrial suburbs to have the lowest school rates.

Analysis of Rate Behavior

The previous chapters provide the means for interpreting the tax rate movements just noted. The fact, for example,

4. Joseph R. Lamping, "Fragmentation," Mimeographed (Milwaukee: Milwaukee Department of Community Development, 1956), p. 8.

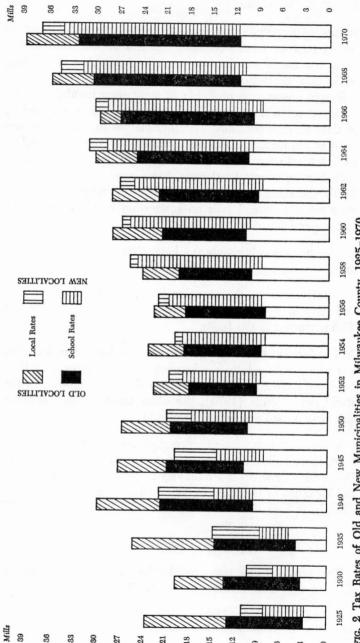

FIG. 2 Tax Rates of Old and New Municipalities in Milwaukee County, 1925–1970.

that school tax rates rose while local rates fell during the last 25 years should come as no surprise. Chapter 6 detailed the sharp increase in educational expenditures since 1945, especially in the suburbs. Since this local service is financed almost entirely by property taxes, and since educational costs rose faster than property values, obviously school rates had to go up. That is, per capita property valuation for the suburbs increased fivefold between 1945 and 1970, whereas school costs increased an amazing elevenfold.

Noneducational expenditures do not depend nearly so much on the property tax. Thus, the growth in the state shared taxes, coupled with extensive use of special assessments and subdivision building requirements, made it possible to lower the average local rate in spite of a rise in per capita noneducational expenditures. Local tax rates were found to have no correlation with per capita noneducational expenditures in recent years, but these rates did have a definite correlation with state payments. A key factor is the fact that income taxes are shared with local municipal governments, not with school districts. Thus the growth in shared tax dollars can be expected to relieve pressure on the local tax rate rather than the school tax rate—exactly what the data reveal.

On the surface, at least, it is clear why the central city has a local rate so much higher than its suburbs: it has high per capita expenditures and low per capita resources compared with the suburban average. It is somewhat more complicated to explain why the resources are low and why the expenditures are high, but given those facts, the explanation of the high local rate is simple.

Any tax rate has to be read in the light of several factors or qualifications before it takes on any real meaning. Some of the weightier factors are: per capita tax base, per capita expenditures, outside revenue sources (especially shared taxes in Wisconsin), quality of local services (including education), willingness to borrow, other local revenues (e.g., special assessments, fees, etc.), and general economic conditions (war, depression, inflation, etc.).

Thus, for example, how is one to interpret the fact that

a certain locality has a very small local rate? It could mean any of the following things: very few or very inferior local services, very high revenues from other sources, or a very high property base per capita. As a matter of fact, Franklin in 1925 and Fox Point in 1962 did both have very low local rates. But what a difference! Franklin provided few services in 1925 (and those without frills); also, it had few outside revenue sources. Fox Point in 1962, on the other hand, supplied high quality services, spent generously per capita, and had a notably high source of outside revenue. Similarly, Milwaukee and Greenfield had the two highest total rates in the county in 1960. How completely fallacious it would be to conclude that their revenue and spending patterns resembled one another. Milwaukee spent four times as much per capita as Greenfield on noneducational services that year.

Another hint of the mistake of interpreting tax rates by themselves grows out of the entire investigation about greater or lesser fiscal homogeneity. This chapter unfolded a very notable movement toward uniformity in total tax rates. One might be tempted to see therein a manifestation of increasing uniformity in expenditures and resources, since tax rates supposedly express a relation between these two. As a matter of fact, what we found was this: a move toward greater uniformity in noneducational expenditures per capita from 1956 on; little change either way in per capita educational expenditures and in property values; a slight move away from uniformity in the matter of state payments. For that reason, the growing homogeneity of total tax rates has been interpreted in terms of two pressures: the political pressure in localities that already had high tax rates to restrain further expansion and the pressure in all localities to spend more dollars on education, for reasons that are both quantitative (more school age children) and qualitative (better teacher salaries, fewer children per classroom, new programs, etc.)

With all the necessary qualifications made, however, tax rates surely do tell us something. Thus, they supply a hint, at least, of local burden. Generally—and, I think, with good reason—we think of the property tax burden in terms of taxes on housing. To be sure, mercantile and manufacturing property taxes are very real, but the discussion of burden is more properly confined to persons, and, therefore, to residential property. Even granting the increased importance of intangible wealth, and even granting the merits of income as a measure of ability, it still seems safe to assume at least a rough relation of proportionality between one's shelter payments and one's general ability to pay. It has meaning, then, to say that those who pay high rates have a heavy burden and those with low rates have a light burden. In this connection, the finding of a strong trend toward uniformity in total tax rates can be interpreted as a move toward more equal burdens.

Many people fail to realize that renters, along with homeowners, pay residential property taxes. Studies have revealed that roughly the same proportion of a renter's shelter payments go into property taxes (through the landlord) as do the shelter payments of a person living in his own home. This has particular significance for central cities in three ways: central cities generally have higher local taxes than suburbs; proportionately more central city households live in rented quarters than do suburban households; and, as a group, the poor tend to live in rental housing more than the middle and upper income groups do. This last point brings the discussion squarely back to the relation between tax rates and burden.

One commentator remarked that residential property taxes were financing only 29 percent of Milwaukee's city and school expenditures in 1960, while 32 percent of its money was coming from industrial and mercantile property.[5] In the context of our present discussion of burden, it could be misleading to say that "only" 29 percent of local expenditures were financed by residential property taxes. The real question of burden is not what kind of property mix a locality has, but how much tax must be paid per $1,000 of property. Thus, in 1960, Milwaukee's 741,324 residents were paying higher

5. *The Milwaukee Journal*, 20 September 1960.

rates of tax on shelter than any other citizens of Milwaukee County in spite of the fact that their residential property taxes paid for "only" 29 percent of city and school outlays.

It is obvious that different communities receive different quantities and qualities of public service even when the tax rates are the same. And yet, it still makes sense to speak of heavy or light burden directly in terms of high or low rates. That is, since the existence and size of tax payments are so largely compulsory, since the voting power of the individual taxpayer does not supply him with any thing like the free choice of his private market purchases, and since the freedom of movement from one locality to another is a highly limited freedom, it would seem that there is a sense in which tax rates and tax burdens can be roughly equated with one another even independently of the quality of services received in return.

To the extent that the above is true, we can venture the following statements about the present situation in Milwaukee County regarding tax burdens:

1. The central city has a higher burden than its suburbs in local and in total rates.

2. The older localities (especially those with a fairly solid industrial base) have a higher burden in local rates.

3. The younger localities have had a higher burden in school rates since 1952.

4. The heavily industrial localities have a lighter school and a lighter total burden than all others.

5. The residential localities have a heavier school burden.

Tables were prepared expressing total expenditures per $1,000, (i.e., relating the sum of educational and noneducational expenditures to property tax base). These figures tell with considerable precision what tax rates would be if all expenditures were paid for out of property resources. Since the trend is for property taxes to supply a smaller and smaller percentage of total revenue,[6] the decision was made not to include this hypothetical information. Preliminary analysis indicated, however, that the ranking of localities according to expenditures per $1,000 resembles the ranking according to tax rates both for noneducational expenditures and for total expenditures.

After the above approach had been dropped, another method was chosen for filling out the picture given by tax rates. The total of the state payments covered in Chapter 5 was divided by the property base of each locality for each time period. These figures tell how many equivalent mills the locality has to start out with before it comes to levying its property tax. That is, they tell how much less property tax has to be levied thanks to state assistance. The results, expressed as mills, are given in Table 32. Inasmuch as these state payments are used almost exclusively for noneducational purposes, it would be of considerable interest to relate them to local tax rates. For that reason, in each column of Table 32 are listed the equivalent number of mills provided by state payments, and in parentheses next to each is the actual local tax rate (from Table 27) for the same locality in that year. For both, the rate is rounded off to the nearest mill.

One clear conclusion from the table is that the wealthy residential suburbs and the major "utility plant suburb" fare best in this respect. Or put another way, if we were to assume that spending habits would not change, it would be these two groups of suburbs which would have to increase their local tax rates the most in the event of the withdrawal of state payments. As a matter of fact, when localities are ranked according to the number of mills they save as a result of state funds, they come out similar to their ranking in terms of per capita dollar amounts of state money. The one notable difference is that the industrial enclaves rank high in per capita dollar terms but low in millage terms. The reason, of course, is that their high state payments per capita are

6. Alan K. Campbell and Seymour Sacks, *Metropolitan America* (New York: The Free Press, 1967), p. 13.

TABLE 32
Property Tax Rate Equivalents of State Payments for Municipalities of Milwaukee County, 1960–1970

	1960	1962	1964	1966	1968	1970
Milwaukee	6(11)[a]	6(13)	7(13)	8(14)	8(15)	8(15)
Bayside	9(1)	9(1)	8(2)	10(0)	11(2)	10(2)
Brown Deer	4(2)	5(3)	6(2)	6(2)	5(4)	6(3)
Cudahy	4(7)	5(6)	5(6)	5(3)	6(4)	5(6)
Fox Point	12(1)	12(1)	10(1)	12(1)	14(1)	11(0)
Franklin	6(0)	6(2)	8(0)	8(2)	9(3)	8(3)
Glendale	5(1)	6(1)	6(0)	6(1)	7(1)	5(2)
Greenda'e	5(2)	5(2)	6(2)	6(2)	6(3)	6(3)
Greenfield	5(1)	5(2)	6(2)	6(1)	7(2)	6(3)
Hales Corners	5(1)	6(1)	7(1)	7(2)	7(3)	7(2)
Oak Creek	28(0)	30(0)	30(0)	31(0)	25(0)	23(0)
River Hills	19(0)	18(1)	13(2)	13(3)	16(3)	14(2)
St. Francis	10(2)	9(3)	10(4)	11(6)	10(6)	12(7)
Shorewood	10(4)	10(5)	9(6)	11(5)	10(6)	10(6)
S. Milwaukee	5(9)	4(9)	6(7)	8(5)	7(6)	7(6)
Wauwatosa	7(2)	6(3)	7(4)	7(3)	7(3)	7(3)
W. Allis	5(9)	4(11)	5(11)	6(10)	6(10)	6(10)
W. Milwaukee	5(1)	4(3)	4(3)	5(3)	4(5)	3(7)
Whitefish Bay	11(1)	10(1)	10(2)	10(2)	10(3)	9(2)
Suburbs	7(4)	6(5)	7(5)	8(4)	8(4)	7(5)
Total County	7(9)	6(10)	7(10)	8(10)	8(11)	8(11)

Sources: State of Wisconsin, Office of Tax Commission, Assessors of Incomes Statistical Report of Property Valuations for the County of Milwaukee for respective years; author's calculations from data presented in Tables 2, 5, 7, 8, and 9.

[a] The figures in parentheses show actual local property tax rates.

outweighed by their very high property value per capita. Thus, they are almost embarrassed by their riches. They have a rich property base to call on, but their state payments are so large that they do not feel the need to tap it heavily for noneducational purposes. "Predominantly industrial enclaves, where manufacturing plants provide revenue windfalls, may become financial oases, literally unable to prevent their tax rates from falling no matter how lavish their public budgets become."[7]

This leads to an important reminder for interpreting Table 32. The number of mills that a municipality "saves" because of state payments depends on how many tax dollars each mill brings in. The city of St. Francis offers a good example. St. Francis saved the equivalent of 12 mills in 1970 as a result of the money it received from the state. This is well above the average for the 19 municipalities. Why did St. Francis save so much? Simply because it had the lowest per capita property values in the whole county that year. Each mill raises very few dollars in St. Francis. In other words, even though its per capita amount of state payments was below the suburban average, each dollar of those state funds would have been unusually difficult for St. Francis to raise from its own property tax base. Only in this sense does this hard-pressed city (with the highest suburban total tax rate in the county), obtain a better "break" than normal from state payments.

The relatively unfortunate position of the central city is seen from another reading of the data in Table 32. Over the years, Milwaukee's property tax "saving" from state payments has been far less than its actual local rates (the figures in parentheses); in the suburbs, on the other hand, the average saving has been more than the actual rate, at least since 1945. Thus, even though the table has already made allowance for the central city's lower property value per capita, (recall the illustration of St. Francis), its relative position still remains inferior.

The older suburbs with more balance in their property uses are in a position quite similar to that of the central city. They feel the same pinch in the relation between the number of mills they save through state payments and the number of mills they actually levy in their local rates.

The only group not yet discussed are those younger suburbs whose property is largely devoted to middle income residen-

7. Robert C. Wood, *Metropolis Against Itself* (New York: Committee for Economic Development, 1959), p. 24.

tial uses. They are in between the wealthy residential suburbs and the older, more balanced localities. That is, they do not receive so many mills from the state as do the former, but neither do they demand so much from their residents in actual local rates of tax as do the latter.

Factors Associated With Tax Rates

It should now be possible to make some statements about the factors that apparently influence tax rates in the Milwaukee metropolitan area. Two have already been treated: age and economic character. Another element likely to be influential is population density. Rank correlations indicate there is a positive association between density and local rates. In many time periods the correlation is statistically significant; in others it is strong but not quite significant. Recalling that the older localities are always the most densely populated, we were led to expect such an association from Figure 2. Also, the correlation found between noneducational per capita expenditures and density pointed in this direction. There is this difference, however: the relationship with local tax rates does not fade out in the 1950s the way it did with per capita expenditures. It will be recalled that the services most influential in this correlation are protection and sanitation.

The association between density and school tax rates is quite interesting. There is a very strong positive correlation between these two up through 1950. Thereafter the correlation drops abruptly, then turns negative, and at times becomes significantly negative. The explanation of this sharp turnabout seems to lie in the rates of population growth. This factor apparently outweighs the influence of school size, quality of service, etc.

Another element which might be thought to have an association with tax rates is the amount of local resources (property base plus state payments) in each municipality. Between local rates and resources there is always the expected negative relationship, but the rank coefficients are rarely large enough to be significant. Earlier there was reported a strong and consistent positive correlation between per capita expenditures and per capita resources. Therefore, the negative correlation that now appears suggests either that state payments account for a more than proportionate share of the resources of wealthier localities or that expenditures in wealthier communities do not rise so much as resources. Within Milwaukee County, the correct explanation seems to be a combination of both elements. Rank correlations between resources and school tax rates are quite similar to those between resources and local rates.

Thus, to sum up the influence of resources on tax rates, higher resources in a community generally are associated with both lower local rates and lower school rates. The result is that the wealthier communities pay lower total rates, with the negative correlation between resources and total tax rates becoming significant in many time periods.

It seems plausible that local rates might well rise as population rises. This belief was based on the likelihood that larger numbers of people in a locality would require a greater number of and more complete services. A large population calls for replacement of wells by public water supplies, of septic tanks by a sewage system, of a volunteer fire department by a full-time force, etc. As a matter of fact, there is a positive correlation between population size and local rates which is significant more often than not. School rates and population size show a strong significant positive correlation up into the 1950s; then it drops and turns negative. A major element at work here may well be the disappearance of unincorporated towns. Their traditionally low educational expenditures kept their school rates low, and this helped a great deal in the matching of low rates with small populations. As the towns disappeared in the early 1950s, the municipalities which then emerged at the lower end of the population size list included a number of high income residential suburbs; traditionally, they are big spenders on education. Hence, the turn-around in the correlation coefficients. In this positive association between population size and both kinds of tax rate there is little evidence that economies of scale are operative.

In summary, the following general statements can be made about factors apparently influencing tax rates:

1. Local tax rates are consistently high in localities which are old and which have a large population, high population density, and a property mix well balanced between residential and business uses. These factors, plus others, gave the City of Milwaukee the highest local rates in every single time period.

2. School tax rates are consistently high in the communities which show notable population growth. They undergo sharp changes in their association with population size and with population density.

3. The residential localities regularly have the lowest local rates.

4. Resources are negatively related to local, school, and total rates, but the correlation is rarely significant.

5. School rates are generally highest in the residential suburbs and lowest in the heavily industrialized suburbs.

How explain the first of these points? Apparently, the key to the relation between these older communities and high local rates is the balance of the property base between residential use and business use. No other explanatory factor holds up so well as this; that is, even though age, and population size, and population density have their influence, these latter factors exist often enough in other localities without consistent high local rates. And even among the eight older localities themselves, the causal role of balanced use is clear. Thus West Milwaukee's low local rate is understandable because it certainly does not have the balance we speak of; 80 percent of its property valuation is in the industrial classification. Furthermore, the three older localities which were always residential suburbs (Shorewood, City of Wauwatosa, and Whitefish Bay) have the most normal and average of local rates over the whole five decades; so age is not the explanation. This leaves the other four in the older group—the four with the property balance. The consistency with which they always lead the county in local rates is amazing: during the last 11 time periods these four were the top four out of four on six occasions and none of them ever dropped below seventh.

As a partial explanation of this plight of the balanced communities, it can be argued that a locality with a strong industrial and mercantile property base must supply many and good noneducational services to survive. It would be sheer suicide not to supply industry with plenty of water, sewage facilities, good streets, police protection, fire protection, etc. There is no choice open to either the voters or to the local office-holders in this matter.

In the case of residential communities, however, there is an element of choice. They can, in a sense, afford the luxury of asking themselves: do we want these services? How much of them do we want? The wealthy residential community may decide it wants all of these services and wants a high quality in them; the poorer residential community may decide that it wants less service, either in quantity or quality. In both cases, the local tax rate can be kept low. Examination of noneducational expenditures in Chapter 6 supports this analysis.

Further, in a locality that has a balance of property uses, the per capita value of the residential property is not likely to be very high. That is, the very presence of much industry precludes the possibility of high income homes in the vicinity, unless the industry is isolated or is "light and clean." This fact, coupled with the consistently high population density of these balanced communities, means that the property tax advantage of the industry is pretty well neutralized by lower residential property values. But the need for highly developed local services remains. Some confirmation of this last point is found in Margolis's conclusion that: "For dormitory cities household income is higher and density is lower, which explains the failure of balanced cities to derive fiscal advantage from their commercial and industrial properties."[8]

8. Julius Margolis, "Municipal Fiscal Structure in a Metropolitan Region," *The Journal of Political Economy* 65 (June 1957): 231.

8 Infra-Metropolitan Competition

METROPOLITANISM is considered by certain experts in the field to be a problem because of the tension, inefficiency, and inequity that result when an economic unit is artificially divided up into numerous political parts, each pursuing its own self-interest. In public finance terms, a single economic base provides revenues to pay for public services, but crazy-quilt boundary lines divide up the revenues in arbitrary, perverse, and inequitable ways.

Most Milwaukee County municipalities have followed a pattern of narrow self-interest that makes remote the likelihood of voluntary coming together. The parts of this metropolitan area are not only splintered and disunited but also openly competing against one another. Specifically, the competition among the municipalities is for the most profitable land uses and land users. The word "profitable" is used here to imply both the revenue side (per capita property values) and the expenditure side (per capita costs). Thus, for example, a profitable property base would mean as few children as possible per acre, inasmuch as 58 percent of the local expenditures analyzed in Chapter 6 were absorbed by school costs in 1970.

The prudent locality, then, will seek land uses which combine high property valuation with low expenditures. There are two general property classifications which meet these qualifications, either of which can be made the object of zoning regulations. The first is high income residential property with large lots. The fiscal motivations for seeking such property are high tax base per capita, relatively few children per $1,000 of property valuation, no service costs required by industry, and, in Wisconsin, large amounts of shared income tax. The other highly prudent course for the metropolitan locality is to attract a high concentration of business property (commercial and especially industrial). The primary benefit here is a very high property base per capita, relatively low school costs, and, in Wisconsin, generous amounts of shared corporate income tax. The concentration of industrial property must be high enough to offset the disadvantages of supplying public services to industry and of the low value residential property that normally borders industry.

The same financial wisdom dictates that the locality avoid the two following courses. First, a balance between residential and industrial property can be seriously harmful to the local treasury. The presence of a moderate amount of industrial property means relatively small amounts of industrial tax base per capita, low residential values per capita because of proximity to industry, high service levels demanded by the presence of industry, and the likelihood of high density in the residential area with consequent high school costs. The second land use to be avoided is lower middle income residential housing on small building lots; this may take place in a balanced locality or in a purely residential one. The disastrous result in this case is the low property value per capita coupled with high school costs.

No sarcasm is intended in the use of the words "prudent" or "wise" when referring to alternative courses of action. Further, no condemnation of the local officials who follow this wiser course is intended. They have an honest responsibility to their constituents. Given the present system, it would be foolish and indefensible to ask any individual locality (or official) to abandon this responsibility in the name of equity or statesmanship. It would be like asking a successful business firm to be a little less efficient in the name of fairness to its struggling competitor. Speaking of the independent municipalities of a metropolitan area, Wood makes the comment that, "the regional corporations are committed, by statute and financial considerations, to particular solutions of particular problems."[1]

If condemnation be in order, it should be directed at state statutes and state constitutions which foster a system of local governments wherein no recognition is given to the economic unity and interdependence of a metropolitan area. The individual locality has little recourse but to separately seek its own self-interest as do the butcher, baker, and brewer in Adam Smith's celebrated description. This infra-metropolitan competition is more detrimental than simple fragmentation for two reasons. First, in the scramble for limited goods (profitable property tax base) the success of the one locality is at the expense of its neighbor. Second, the common needs and interests of the whole metropolitan area are not only neglected but are directly obstructed.[2] One illustration of the latter in Milwaukee County is the insufficient provision of middle and low income housing, with its consequent bad effect on a balanced labor force.[3]

The Wisconsin shared income tax will be omitted from the following examination. Its inclusion would obviously make the case far easier to prove. Nonetheless, the search for competition, or municipal mercantilism, has been limited to the property tax base in order that the findings may possess more universality and be applicable to metropolitan areas outside of Wisconsin. The question being posed is this: do the overt actions of the municipalities accord with the prudent courses described above? If they do, it suggests support for the hypothesis of infra-metropolitan competition.

To make the investigation more concrete and objective,

1. Robert C. Wood, *Metropolis Against Itself* (New York: Committee for Economic Development, 1959), p. 32.

2. Wilfred Owen, *Cities in the Motor Age* (New York: Viking Press, 1959), p. 139. The author makes the point that the metropolitan areas do not suffer from mere apathy but from resistance to any serious effort at cooperation.

3. Metropolitan Study Commission, *An Analysis of Land Use and Zoning in Milwaukee County, Wisconsin* (Milwaukee: MSC, 1959), p. v.

the following illustrations will be confined to zoning regulations which accord with the prudent courses outlined above, and to official municipal actions clearly based on considerations of profitable property uses. Many other actions, therefore, will be omitted even though they harmonize well with the hypothesis of infra-metropolitan competition. For example, the fact that 11 different localities in Milwaukee County have added to their area since 1950 is almost surely a part of this competition; nonetheless, these annexation activities will not be included. Similarly, no reference will be made to the normal, day-by-day efforts of localities to attract industry into their borders by establishment of Economic Development Commissions, special tax breaks, etc.

Since infra-metropolitan competition is being analyzed in terms of property tax base, much of the evidence is to be found in the zoning ordinances of the municipalities. They constitute the obvious instruments of land use control. Fortunately, a zoning and land use study was made in 1958 by the Metropolitan Study Commission, an impartial body established by the Wisconsin state legislature for studying the needs and problems of Milwaukee County.[4] This chapter makes considerable use of their material.

The localities fall into natural groupings. First, there are the three "utility suburbs." In view of the Wisconsin system of sharing utility taxes it is a decisive advantage for a locality to have a large utility plant within its borders. The competition for such property in Milwaukee County makes an exciting story. For decades, the town of Lake possessed the major utility plant of the whole area. The town benefited richly in shared utility taxes from the state and was anxious to preserve its bonanza. It was especially hostile to the city of Milwaukee in view of the latter's annexation policy and strove to protect its big revenue-producer from the central city. But then the part of the town immediately surrounding the utility plant incorporated itself as the city of St. Francis in 1951. Ironically, Lake felt it could not continue without its utility

4. Ibid. The Committee prepared a valuable atlas to accompany the *Analysis*, wherein appear detailed land use maps and zoning maps.

income and therefore agreed to consolidate entirely with its old foe Milwaukee.

As noted in Chapter 3, Oak Creek wrote the other chapter in competition for utility windfall payments. When the Wisconsin Electric Power Company started construction of an enormous power plant within the borders of rural Oak Creek, the town citizens recognized the two "dangers" of either losing the plant to a neighboring municipality by annexation or having the area immediately around the plant incorporate as St. Francis did. To head off these threats, the town accomplished the impressive feat of inducing the state legislature to change the requirements for incorporation (the "Oak Creek Law"). Dollar figures in Chapter 5 indicate how handsomely the move paid off. Thus, one town (Lake) went out of existence, one town (Oak Creek) had state legislation passed to permit it to become a city, and a new locality (St. Francis) came into being—all as a result of competition for utility property.

Another aspect of the infra-metropolitan competition for property is the search for a strong industrial tax base. The simple belief of an earlier day that any industrial property was automatically good for local public finances has been greatly modified. Modern wisdom dictates that a jurisdiction should either have no industry inside its borders or else lots of it. The two prime illustrations of competition for industrial property in Milwaukee County are the village of West Milwaukee and the city of Glendale. (Oak Creek, especially in recent years, would be a third example; however, its utility coup overshadows its successful attraction of manufacturing firms.) West Milwaukee was incorporated in 1906. From the time it originally formed itself around an industrial plant, West Milwaukee has steadfastly pursued a policy of encouraging industrial location and growth within its borders. Through annexation it expanded those borders by half during the 1950s and yet, actually dropped in population during the decade because the new land was zoned for manufacturing purposes. As a result, 80 percent of West Milwaukee's taxable property was in the manufacturing category by 1970, and the village had $43,000 per capita property valuation that year as compared with a county average of $8,000 per capita.

The other example of a wholehearted search for industrial property is the city of Glendale. This municipality was incorporated precisely for the purpose of garnering a large industrial tax base (see p. 33). Glendale has so zoned its land that it clearly is aiming at maintaining its initial advantage. In 1970, the city had $20,000 property valuation per capita as compared with the $8,000 county average; about 60 percent of it was in nonresidential property. At least three other localities were incorporated at the turn of the century around industrial complexes (Cudahy, West Allis, and South Milwaukee) and sought to attract industry afterward, but their history does not show the clear-cut competitive behavior being analyzed in this section.

That makes five localities whose clear and open policy was the acquisition for themselves of a profitable property base. There is more of the same. Presently, three very high income residential suburbs are to be found in Milwaukee County: River Hills, Fox Point, and Bayside. In each decennial census these three are consistently listed as having the highest median family income of the county localities. By very stringent zoning regulations they have permanently guaranteed for themselves a high property tax base per capita. The zoning ordinances permit no industrial land use at all, provide for practically no commercial land use (3 percent of the land is zoned for this use in one locality, 2 percent in another, and none in the third), insist on very large building lots, and control in varying degrees the kind of residences to be built. The result: these three have the highest per capita residential property valuations in the county in 1970 and, along with the two industrial suburbs just considered, have the highest total property base per capita in the county. There is no evidence that the overpowering motive of these three communities was the acquisition of a rich tax base. There is, however, abundant evidence that they clearly and consistently pursued a policy of permitting certain kinds of land uses (which were fiscally profitable) and forbidding other kinds of land uses (which were fiscally unprofitable); in a metropolitan setting, such a policy is certainly a form of competition.

Then, there are other municipalities that manifest their familiarity with the prudence of local public finance by trying to imitate the three exclusive suburbs just examined. They are Franklin, Greendale, Hales Corners, and Oak Creek. Although these four have not drawn large numbers of wealthy residents as yet, they are at least making sure of avoiding the financial burden of high density, low income residential development through their insistence on large building lots. With the exception of Oak Creek, they are also imitating the high income residential suburbs by zoning very little land for industrial uses (5 percent in Greendale, 2 percent in both Franklin and Hales Corners). The requirement that new homes be built on large lots already seems to be paying off; three of the four municipalities had, between 1960 and 1970, climbed a few notches when the county localities are ranked by per capita residential property values.

And finally, there are two localities which show some characteristics of the "new wisdom" and some characteristics of the old—Shorewood and Whitefish Bay. Incorporated around the turn of the century, they passed comprehensive zoning ordinances (1919 and 1922, respectively) that assured their development as purely residential suburbs. This move, coupled with the fact that only the well-to-do moved to suburbia at that time, shows signs of the more modern wisdom in this matter. But their failure to insist on large building lots, thereby avoiding high density development, is less in line with today's financial prudence. In spite of this lapse, they still hold the fourth and seventh positions today among the 19 municipalities in per capita residential tax base.

This leaves only seven localities in the county which have not joined vigorously in the competition. Four of them (including the central city) are older, balanced localities which for a long time have not had choice in the overall direction of their land use development. The refined use of zoning in infra-metropolitan competition is a relatively modern phenomenon and these latter localities had already gone too far to change. Their balance between industrial, mercantile, and residential land uses characterized most municipalities during the years of their youth. Today's generation of metropolitan localities are characterized by specialization of land use, or what the Land Use and Zoning Committee of the Metropolitan Study Commission calls "internal homogeneity as to land use types."[5]

In the case of Milwaukee County, therefore, there appears to be considerable support for the hypothesis of infra-metropolitan competition. Of the 20 county localities studied, 13 were found to be acting in accord with the hypothesis; there were four whose "existing plant facilities" made entry into the race impossible, leaving only three who do not show signs of active engagement. Furthermore, the trend indicates that things are getting worse—worse in the sense that the competition itself shows real signs of growing stronger and sharper since 1950. This is especially so in the wholesale swing to regulations insisting on large building lots and in the general increase in land use specialization. Worse also in the sense that the economic unity and interdependence of the metropolitan area (of which the increasing specialization can be viewed as a manifestation) is growing at the very time that this competition is growing. Thus, as the need for shared responsibility, for recognition of mutual interest, and for united action increases, their likelihood decreases. It decreases because it is the essence of competition that each party sees his own welfare as somehow opposed to the welfare of his competitors. Treating this same general question 25 years ago, Henry Fagin predicted a growth in this kind of competition and a growth in inequality as a result. As he then noted, "it is in the nature of most of the measures available to local government that they are most effective in exaggerating rather than correcting uneven distributions."[6] Another fact that

5. Ibid., p. iii.
6. Henry Fagin, "Financing Municipal Services in a Metropolitan Region," *Journal of the American Institute of Planners* 19 (Fall 1953), p. 218.

emerges is the extent to which competitive fragmentation occurs among the suburbs themselves. This aspect of the problem is often overlooked in the stress put on the disparities and disunity between the central city and its satellite area.

To return, then, to the central question of the entire study, there is a diminishing foundation for hope that the parts of the metropolitan area will spontaneously increase their cooperation or integration. Similarly, voluntary metropolitan coordination is not a promising solution to the sickness of our large cities.

9 Findings and Implications

NO EFORT will be made here to summarize the data of the earlier chapters. The purpose is rather to put together the major pieces into a composite picture. Over the past 50 years, the municipalities of Milwaukee County have grown more like one another in some respects but not in others. Their overall spending patterns show a modest movement toward homogeneity in the last 10 or 12 years. The property tax rates of the 19 municipalities reveal a much more pronounced coming together over the entire period of the study. The fiscal capacity of the localities, however, has not shown any tendency toward similarity. In fact, resources seemed to be even more unevenly distributed in 1970 than in 1920. Neither in per capita property values, nor in the pattern of state payments is there anything to suggest a lessening of resource variation in the future.

The answer, therefore, to the central question to the study is clear: there are no fiscal grounds for expecting the municipalities of this metropolitan area spontaneously to move toward greater coordination. To put it another way, there are no indications that the metropolitan problem (governmental balkanization of an economic unity) is solving itself. On the one hand, fiscal disparities are a major part of that problem and the pivotal kind of disparity (resources) is not lessening. On the other hand, these same disparities provide strong motivation for some municipalities to retain the splintered status quo and thereby retain the metropolitan problem. Therefore,

153

there are no grounds for hoping that spillovers will diminish over time, or that wasteful duplications will disappear, or that efficiency will increase through economies of scale, or that narrow bickering and competition will lessen, or that coordinated treatment of areawide problems will emerge. The financial data and trends uncovered in this study work against any functional or governmental coordination within the Milwaukee metropolitan area.

The basis of so pessimistic a conclusion is twofold. First, relatively high fiscal capacity is the one advantage that a community will not willingly forego; therefore, the growing variation in resources is discouraging. Secondly, the slight shift toward more similarity in per capita expenditures makes the probability of voluntary coordination even more unlikely. The reason, again, is related to the widening spread in resources. The coming together in spending patterns results from the growing urbanization of the whole county. As towns disappeared, the extent and quality of public services in these rural sections of the county drew closer to the sections already urbanized. Resource-rich municipalities noticed the needs and spending levels of poorer localities drawing closer to their own, making them less likely than ever to integrate with these "underdeveloped" municipalities. Thus, self-interest suggested to the wealthy communities that increasing uniformity of expenditures was a reason for opposing fiscal unification. Put another way, it would require less altruism for a well-endowed municipality to share with a poor neighbor who spent little than to share with a poor neighbor whose spending was on the upswing.

Tax rates offer a mixed picture. Growing uniformity of total tax rates might at first suggest an increasing similarity of burden, and, therefore, be thought of as an encouraging factor for the cause of integration. If the coming together of total rates were a manifestation of growing similarity of local needs, the picture would, indeed, be bright. If it means, however, that wealthier communities spend more simply because of their affluence, the picture is dark. The consistently high correlation found between expenditures and resources testifies that this darker view is the correct one. Hence, integration is seen by rich communities as something to be opposed, for it would end the high quality services that their generous spending permits. The hopes for cooperation that the trend of total tax rates might raise are further dimmed by the fact that local tax rates (the only ones that municipal governments directly control) still show extremely wide variation.

The second major question of the investigation dealt with the relationship over time between the central city and its suburbs. Until 1956, per capita expenditures of Milwaukee had regularly been higher than the suburban average; since that date, the suburbs have been spending more. Is this trend favorable or unfavorable for Milwaukee? In the absence of any way of measuring service quality, the question does not permit an unequivocal answer. It was also found that the central city's total property tax rates have always been higher than the suburban average (about one-third higher during the 1960s) and that this divergence has been widening of late. Is this trend favorable or unfavorable for Milwaukee? It is rather safe in this case to say that it is unfavorable for the central city, especially since the expenditure figures indicate that the city probably receives poorer services in return for its heavier tax burden. And, finally, there is the matter of fiscal capacity or resources. The central city's overall position has always been inferior to the suburbs, and that inferior position has been worsening. This overall picture is true of both capacity components—property values and state payments. Clearly, then, the likelihood of any voluntary sharing or coordination between Milwaukee and the rest of the county is minimal. If, as seems likely, the Milwaukee situation is typical, the outlook for America's big city sickness is bleak.

Beyond these two major conclusions—both of them pessimistic—there were other broad findings worthy of comment. The evidence of narrow self-interest on the part of most county municipalities (Chapter 8) makes spontaneous coordination still more unlikely. To expect meaningful fiscal sharing in the face of such overt fiscal mercantilism is surely to dwell in a dream world. Going one step further, the hostility engendered by 11 municipalities aggressively scrambling for annexable land during the 1950s makes the chances of voluntary coming together more remote. Nor is that the end of the dreary litany. All of the foregoing took place within a fixed geographical area. If the boundaries of the metropolitan area had been re-defined each decade to embrace more and more communities, the outlook would be even more dismal.

Large lot residential zoning is another historical trend affecting the public finances in the Milwaukee area. Aside from it being a manifestation of fiscal "prudence," this growing practice forces low income people into a relatively few municipalities—those that were "imprudent." This latter effect suggests a hastening of the central city's fiscal deterioration, and a widening of the property tax disparities between the county's rich and poor localities. Finally, it appears that most fringe communities are imitating the large lot practice; this bodes ill for the future.

Municipal specialization of land use, it was found, is not only prevalent but growing dramatically. It is, of course, the presence of a large unified economic base which, along with mobility, makes specialization possible. The underlying unity makes the specialized municipal pieces very interdependent. Yet, as far as local finances are concerned, the surface appearance of independence which municipal borders permit is far more decisive than the real economic unity existing just below the surface.

An odd aspect of this contradiction is that all the forces, the motives, the rewards, the competitiveness of the private sector of the economy are thereby introduced into the public sector. Yet, the reason most local governmental services exist is because the private sector could not do the job. This puts Americans in an embarrassing position. Since the reason for moving protection and recreation and education out of the private sector into the public sector was to make them available equally to all our citizens, we feel compelled to pretend that this result actually takes place. The earlier chapters of this study show how unreal this pretense is in at least one of the nation's larger metropolitan areas.

The range of fiscal disparities among Milwaukee metropolitan jurisdictions was impressive as late as 1970. One municipality had a local tax rate 153 times as large as another. One municipality had per capita property valuation eight times that of another. There was a 6 to 1 spread even in per capita state payments—the one revenue source wherein a more equal distribution might have been expected. The total per capita expenditures of one municipality were six times as large as those of another. The spread was 5 to 1 in spending on so basic a function as education.

The resource disparities can be looked at from the opposite side, by viewing changes that would result from ironing out the differences. In that event, there would have been a per capita amount of $459.48 available to each municipality in 1970 to spend on local services. The present 7.5 to 1 spread in total resources would be wiped out. The community that is presently richest would see a 510 percent drop in its wealth, whereas the one that is now poorest would see its resources increase by an impressive 44 percent. The central city, to which the majority of dollars would go in any such averaging scheme, would see its resources increase from $402.58 per person to $459.48. In view of Milwaukee's unusually burdensome property tax rates and in view of the services it provides every day to citizens of every county municipality, perhaps a case could be made for such a sharing scheme.

Overall, one can summarize the previous findings by saying that the system of local government in America's metropolitan areas is out of line with economic reality. Since Wisconsin is not fundamentally different from the other 49 states in this respect, it is fair to speak of America rather than of Milwaukee County alone. The year 1920 was deliberately chosen as the starting point of the study because it comes close to marking the start of the automobile era and therefore, the start of the metropolitan era. The historical examination revealed that governmental changes have simply failed to keep up with the economic changes that took place over the past five decades. It does not seem to be a glib generalization to say that the local governments in Milwaukee County are expected to perform as though they were still geographically isolated and economically independent localities.

The data of earlier chapters provide a basis for policy decisions. No more than a few hints will be suggested here. Although the study focused on Milwaukee County, the policy implications seem applicable to most metropolitan areas.

The city of Milwaukee will almost surely continue fiscally to deteriorate. This may not be so terrible in terms of employment; most new job openings are in the suburbs. It will, however, be terrible for the people left within the city borders. It appears that they will live in an increasingly unpleasant environment, bear higher and higher tax burdens, and receive for their trouble poorer and poorer services. The trends of the last 50 years point that way. There is no local machinery for reversing that trend; therefore, Milwaukee should stop pretending that it is fiscally viable and it should stop blaming the suburbs for its plight. It is at the state capitol that the decision will be made whether to let the central city continue its decline (by maintaining present policies) or to make a change.

A second policy implication touches on the issue of home rule and local autonomy. The concept of local autonomy is a dead relic of an earlier age insofar as it assumes each metropolitan jurisdiction can provide basic public services with reasonably fair tax burdens. The concept is very much alive, however, insofar as it holds that every jurisdiction (whether in a metropolitan area or not) should do so. Only the state legislature can resolve this contradiction between "can" and "should."

Education is widely considered to be the most important local governmental service; as the earlier data showed, it is certainly the most expensive service. In the past, the state government of Wisconsin forced considerable consolidation of school districts, not without much opposition and bitterness. Yet, in 1970, even within a single urbanized county we find numerous independent districts with widely different fiscal profiles. Should the state continue to push consolidation within Milwaukee County? The wide fiscal variations in education that were uncovered in this study indicate that more consolidation is in order, perhaps to the point of a single countywide school tax base. In addition, the notable growth in similarity of school tax rates knocks down one barrier in the way of further consolidation. The three big barriers remaining are attachment to local control, different levels of quality (as indicated by per pupil spending levels), and reluctance to see racial and economic integration in the schools. The question could conceivably be dealt with by cooperative action on the part of individual school districts and individual city school boards, but realistically nothing will be done below the state level. We are reminded by the 1971 California experience that if the state legislature will not deal with the issue the state courts may do it instead.

Finally, the major policy implication of this study is that the state government has failed in the statutory and constitutional responsibilities it has toward local governments. Rich rhetoric about home rule charters or about a tradition of decentralized government can not undo the verdict of neglect and failure. Although it is Wisconsin that sits in the defendant's box in the present study, it appears that the same condemnatory judgment could be passed, in varying degrees, on every other state government, with the possible exception of Hawaii. Dillon's rule, which states that grants of power by states to municipalities are to be interpreted narrowly, simply reflects prevailing practice in this country.[1] State constitutions are clear on the point that local governments are creatures of the state and that the police power is vested in the state government. And they leave no doubt that it is the state (not the local municipality or district) that is ultimately responsible for seeing that adequate education is provided to all its citizens. And so on.

There is no evidence in this study that Wisconsin's local governmental structure necessarily has to be overhauled. There is, however, abundant evidence that the present system

---

1. John F. Dillon, *Commentaries on the Law of Municipal Corporations* (5th ed.; Boston, 1911), p. 448.

of paying for local services in metropolitan areas is difficult to justify. Naturally, it is not the existence of differences in wealth that is objectionable. Perhaps, in a different institutional framework, it would even be possible to condone the fact that these fiscal disparities result in widely different levels of service and widely different burdens. In the present framework, however, wherein the parent state has the responsibility to see that the services are adequately and equitably provided to all its citizens, the wide variation in service quality and in burden can not be condoned. When this failure of the state to meet its responsibilities occurs in an economically unified region called a metropolitan area, the status quo becomes harder to defend. Finally, when the state government distributes payments to local governments in a way that magnifies the original disparities, the verdict becomes inescapable.

It would be presumptuous to indicate which of the many forms of redress would be best. The dedicated state officials of Wisconsin are most qualified to make that determination. All that this investigation contributes is a documentation of the twin facts that there exist wide differences among Milwaukee County municipalities in tax burden and in service quality, and that the history of the past five decades offers no basis for expecting those differences to lessen or go away in the absence of state action.

Index

DESIGNED BY GARY GORE
COMPOSED, PRINTED, AND BOUND BY
THE MAPLE PRESS CO., INC., YORK, PENNSYLVANIA
TEXT LINES ARE SET IN LINOTYPE CALEDONIA,
DISPLAY LINES IN CRAW MODERN

Library of Congress Cataloging in Publication Data
Curran, Donald J   1926–
Metropolitan financing.
Includes bibliographical references.
1. Finance, Public—Milwaukee. I. Title.
HJ9340.M5C86   336.775'95   72-7984
ISBN 0-299-06290-2